FORMULA 1
THE PURSUIT OF SPEED

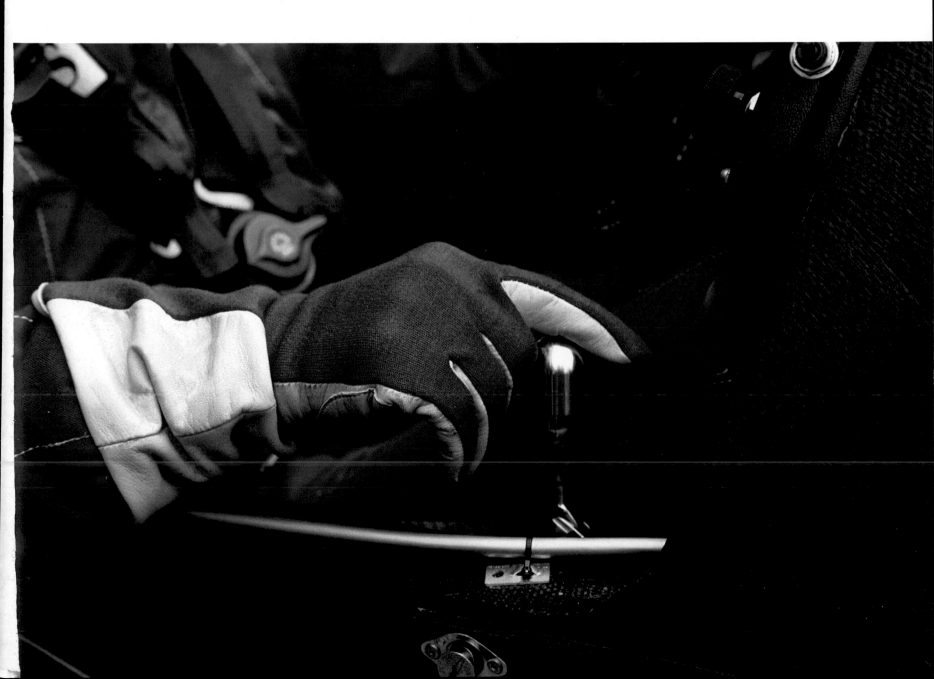

FORMULA 1
THE PURSUIT OF SPEED

photography by **Paul-Henri** & **Bernard Cahier**
words by **Maurice Hamilton**

Aurum
Press

The pictures in this book are the work of a father and son photographic dynasty, and *The Pursuit of Speed* is the result of a project I had been wanting to do for quite a long time. A book that would blend and showcase the work that my late father and I have completed during the past sixty-four years in the extraordinary world of Formula One Grand Prix Racing (F1), a body of work that comprises what is known as The Cahier Archive.

So when I was contacted by Lucy Warburton from Aurum Press, telling me she had a book idea on the inside world of F1, I thought to myself that this could be a great opportunity. But selecting the relevant pictures from a collection of well over half-a-million photographs was no easy task. The tremendous evolution of both men and machines, from the glorious days of true camaraderie and endless tragedy to today's world of high-tech show, had to be blended into a coherent, harmonious and beautiful book. That was indeed a challenge, and the result is here, for your viewing pleasure. I hope you will enjoy reading the work as much as we have relished putting it together. Motor racing at the highest level is all about addiction to speed; it is the dance of life and death on the very edge of sanity. Intense emotions, unlimited courage, outrageous dexterity, powerful rivalries: all are blended in *The Pursuit of Speed*, and the result is a sort of visual symphony of this unique spectacle. My dad would be very proud.

CONTENTS

SIR JACKIE STEWART OBE

It's seldom in any business, sport or the world of entertainment, that sons become as successful as their fathers; but Paul-Henri Cahier has achieved this feat.

When I entered Formula One Grand Prix racing, Bernard Cahier was already one of the most globally recognised journalists and photographers in motorsport. As I write this foreword, Paul-Henri enjoys the same impressive presence and respect as an F1 photographer.

Bernard Cahier became more than a journalist and a photographer, even though he was hardly ever to be seen without a camera around his neck. He wrote for many of the top motorsport magazines in the world and beyond that, he had commercial relationships with companies such as Goodyear, in which he served at the highest level, including as President and Chairmen. Bernard's presence in the sport is further noted by his advisory role on the ground-breaking film on Formula One, *Grand Prix* by John Frankenheimer. Bernard even featured in the film from time to time.

It was Bernard's close relationship to many of the top drivers that stood him apart and produced such resonating photographs. One of whom was Baron de Graffenried, known to his friends as *Toulo*. It is amazing how serendipitous life can be. When I was driving F1 cars, Bernard took me to Toulo's lovely chalet in Villars for lunch. To my absolute amazement, the great Juan Manuel Fangio was at the same table; what a great thrill for a young Grand Prix driver. Even more incredible, that same chalet today belongs to Paul Stewart, my eldest son.

A very important element of the Cahier family partnership was Joan, the wonderful wife of Bernard and mother of Paul-Henri. What a great combination they were and what a wonderful reality that Paul-Henri is today carrying on so successfully the same high skills that he has inherited from his father and mother.

In today's world of photography, Paul-Henri isn't as lucky as his father. I see Paul-Henri at almost every Grand Prix and he is absolutely laden down by huge cameras, extraordinary lenses and the backpack of support equipment required by today's incredibly high standard of photography and definition – rather different to the early days of his art. The combination of two great photographers compiling a book that ranges so widely and demonstrates the immense change that Formula One and motorsport in general has undergone – transforming the look, the speed, the colour and the personality of the sport – is so well revealed in this excellent collection of wonderful photographs.

Formula One: The Pursuit of Speed gives an insight into the world of F1 which few might get to enjoy if it wasn't for the talents of people like Paul-Henri Cahier, Maurice Hamilton and, of course, Bernard Cahier. Bernard was one of the true pioneers of the photographic journey and his and Paul-Henri's work are the reason that we are able to celebrate the world of Formula One.

INTRODUCTION

Sixty-four years is a long time by any standard. In Formula One, the progress and change have been immense. To have this evolution recorded is one thing; to enjoy the benefit of images exquisitely captured on camera is quite another.

That is precisely what we've got between the pages of this book, thanks to the precision, imagination and brilliance of the late Bernard Cahier and his son, Paul-Henri. Between them, father and son have reflected the growth and transformation of a sport that has been glamorous and spectacular throughout.

During this time, and despite enormous evolution, F1's fundamental framework has remained unchanged. The drivers are heroes, no matter what they drive; the rivalries and friendships continue exactly as they were in the 1950s, even if today's enmities are mercilessly exposed by social media.

These central themes are caught perfectly thanks to both photographers enjoying the privilege of being allowed behind the scenes and having the patience to recognise and catch the intimate and tense moments when up close. The subsequent images are unique and priceless.

In the same way that a racing driver's attire defines each era, the size, shape and sophistication of his car marks huge advances in technology across the decades. The teams may have expanded to match this progress but, like the drivers, at heart they remain exactly as they were.

Famous names such as Ferrari, McLaren and Williams continue to be motivated by a massively competitive urge that has not changed regardless of the high-tech trappings. The absolute focus is on finishing first. Second place is no more an option in 2016 than it was in 1956.

The canvas for this thrilling competition has been provided by more than seventy different race tracks since the World Championship began in 1950. And, once again, while the backdrops may have altered in keeping with the necessary demands for safety, the challenge provided by the slow corners and fast curves places the same call for that intoxicating mix of accuracy and daring by the men in their machines.

In the 1950s and 60s, street circuits were more prevalent than today. The images in this book highlight the raw and fairly basic demands placed on drivers by kerbs, lampposts and walls waiting to penalise the smallest error. More recent photographs bring home the understandable need for reducing these hazards while, at the same time, highlighting the sometimes extreme dangers endured decades before. This book brings a striking comparison between these vastly different eras, and only adds to the sense of respect for drivers and their exceptional skills.

When the cars are at rest and crash helmets are removed, there is the opportunity for photographers to capture the more candid moments. The authors have done this with an exquisite stealth that creates the relaxed impression of subjects not being aware of the camera's presence.

At the time of taking each photograph, the focus is literally and naturally on people. But looking at the images with hindsight, a study of the surroundings presents a penetrating portrait of how F1 and its trappings have changed, almost beyond recognition.

From the mechanic in oily overalls with a cigarette and a spanner, to the technicians in crisp uniforms tapping keyboards; from perspiring drivers with grease-stained faces in polo shirts, to today's sponsor-bedecked heroes with shining faces in flameproof overalls; from a kettle and teapot in the back of a shabby truck, to Michelin-inspired cuisine delicately served in air-conditioned business and social enclaves; from team management identified by smart suits and collars and ties, to serious-looking men and women wearing headsets and electronic credentials; all of these arresting comparisons of progress are graphically displayed across the following pages.

If a picture is worth a thousand words, then this book is the photographic equivalent of a major literary work on motor racing at its highest and most dramatic level.

RIVALRIES
THE LEGENDS OF F1

Rivalries exist in motor racing, just as they do in any sport. One competitor wants to beat another. The major difference is that racing drivers are doing it wheel-to-wheel, at anything up to 200mph.

The associated danger is obvious and significant, particularly when defining parameters. A feud will find its limit when physical contact could lead to injury – or worse.

But that does not lessen the impact of searing ambition, as one driver desperately wishes to prove himself faster than another. Sometimes that rival may be in the same team, thereby bringing a further intriguing dimension to a contest that already has a sense of gladiatorial conflict. When Grand Prix drivers don their flameproof overalls and crash helmets bearing personal colours, they are preparing for battle on an asphalt playing field, often with unyielding edges.

The key point – amply illustrated on the following pages – is that the strength and depth of competitiveness has intensified over the decades. Paradoxically, a massive improvement in safety has brought an accompanying increase in potentially threatening enmity. Banging wheels in 2016 leads to outrage and, at worst, a puncture. Sixty years before, such a tactic was guaranteed to end in crash and burn.

More than anything, that thought promoted a sense of family. There was need of it when drivers would perish on an appallingly regular basis. It fostered camaraderie; a sense of belonging and support that is hardly necessary today.

Nonetheless, there were conflicts and jealousies many decades ago. Stirling Moss would irritate his rivals because, as a young upstart, he was fast – and he knew it. Moss fought for the 1958 championship with fellow Englishman, Mike Hawthorn. The duel lasted until the final race, Hawthorn becoming the first British World Champion – but only after the stewards at the Portuguese Grand Prix unsuccessfully tried to exclude Hawthorn on a technicality and, remarkably, Moss had come to his defence. That was the height of 'rivalry' then.

Such gentlemanly conduct continued into the 1960s, particularly at the conclusion of the 1964 championship, which was won by the Briton, John Surtees, after his Ferrari team-mate had hit the back of one of Surtees' rivals. This was accepted, albeit reluctantly, by the aggrieved party as an accident and no more was said in public. Today, there would be stewards' inquiries, court cases and endless social media opinion.

Left
Stirling Moss.

Overleaf
Fellow countrymen tended to stay close. Juan Manuel Fangio *(right)* **and Carlos Menditeguy of Argentina chat before the 1957 French Grand Prix at Rouen-les-Essarts.**

A sharper, potentially corrosive element did not appear until the 1980s, significantly at McLaren when the legendary Ayrton Senna became team-mate to Alain Prost, considered to be one of the best drivers in this or any other decade.

A fight for the 1989 championship between the two ended in a collision while battling for the lead at the penultimate round in Japan. A year later, at the same circuit, Senna simply drove into the back of Prost – now racing for Ferrari – and shoved him off the road, becoming World Champion in the process.

The title battle between Michael Schumacher and Damon Hill in 1994 ended at the final race when the pair collided, popular opinion being that Schumacher caused the crash that eliminated both cars and gave him the championship. Schumacher would go some way to proving he was capable of such a tactic at the final race in 1997 when, once again, he collided with his championship rival, Jacques Villeneuve. This time, Schumacher came off worst in every sense, as he was stripped of his championship points, the title going to Villeneuve.

Schumacher drove for Benetton and Ferrari, while his rivals Hill and Villeneuve raced for Williams. In 2014 and 2015, rivalry returned to within one team as Lewis Hamilton and Nico Rosberg made the most of their technically superior Mercedes to engage in a battle that became increasingly intense. It resulted in a clash of wheels on the track and a frigid atmosphere off it.

At Spa-Francorchamps in 2014, Rosberg was adjudged to have hit the back of Hamilton's car, causing a puncture. A year later, while dominating the championship once more, the pair had edgy moments as they ran wheel-to-wheel on the track – and sometimes off it. Rosberg was not happy when Hamilton cut across to take the lead on the first lap in Japan. The German was even less impressed when the two touched at the first corner of the US Grand Prix, Rosberg being forced to run off the road. Gathering himself together, Rosberg eventually got back in front – only to throw away the lead with an elementary error.

The timing was unfortunate, since the mistake allowed Hamilton to win his second championship in succession. The pair may have been team-mates but there was clearly no love lost in the pre-podium cool-down room when Hamilton playfully threw the cap for second place in Rosberg's direction, only to have it flicked back with barely concealed frustration.

Top row from left
The Grand Prix Drivers' Association emblem on the overalls of Jo Bonnier *(fourth from right)* **indicates how drivers, despite their rivalries, tended to work more closely together in the 1960s. The drivers' briefing before the 1967 German Grand Prix at the Nürburgring** *(left to right)*: **Pedro Rodriguez, Brian Hart, Mike Spence, Jo Siffert, Jacky Ickx, Jackie Stewart, Dan Gurney, Bonnier, Jo Schlesser, Hubert Hahne and Denny Hulme.**

The partnership rivals feared most in the 1960s: Jim Clark *(left)* **and Lotus boss Colin Chapman at Monaco in 1966.**

Middle row from left
Plenty of time to spare before the 1955 Le Mans 24-Hour race. Eugenio Castellotti rests against the rear wheel of his Ferrari and catches up with the news.

Best Man and best mates. Mike Hawthorn *(left)* **and Peter Collins fool around while posing for Bernard Cahier before the wedding of Collins to the American actress Louise King in January 1957. Two years later, both drivers would be dead.**

Bottom row from left
Stirling Moss *(right)* **and Tony Brooks shared the winning Vanwall at Aintree in 1957 to produce the first championship Grand Prix victory for a British car.**

British drivers John Surtees *(left)* **and Jim Clark fought for the championship in 1964, the title going to Surtees.**

That simple impulsive reaction said everything about Rosberg's effort and focus of the previous six months amounting to nothing. Suddenly he was faced with having to do it all over again in 2016; a goal he finally achieved in the last race of the season. Each race must have a winner and a loser in the same way that motor racing is predicated on conflict and barely concealed enmity – just like any other sport.

The fight between Rosberg and Hamilton was nothing new. The difference these days is that the risk element is massively reduced compared to forty years ago. Added to which, the associated action on the track is far more accessible and public than it was in the era virtually free from live television, when drivers might have a difference of opinion, but then politely agree to say no more about it.

But the fact remains that high-fuelled rivalries unique to F1 continue to be at the very core of the sport, as drivers deal with danger while pursuing excellence. Rivalry exists – as it always has done. It's just that the terms of engagement tend to be more dramatically defined at 200mph.

Above left
Signs of the uneasy relationship between McLaren drivers Ayrton Senna *(right)* **and Alain Prost after finishing first and second in the 1988 Hungarian Grand Prix.**

Above right
Team-mates but rivals: Lewis Hamilton *(left)* **and Nico Rosberg of Mercedes stand to attention before a start at Monza in 2015.**

Opposite
The start of an intense and ultimately respectful rivalry as James Hunt scores his first Grand Prix win for Hesketh in the 1975 Dutch Grand Prix, beating the Ferraris of Niki Lauda *(left)* **and Clay Regazzoni.**

Overleaf
There was no rivalry as intense as the in-house fight between McLaren drivers Ayrton Senna (1) and Alain Prost during 1989. The Brazilian leads the Frenchman at Monaco.

■ ASCARI–FARINA
1951

Alberto Ascari and Giuseppe 'Nino' Farina were never great rivals as such, since Ascari usually had the upper hand when racing against a fellow Italian twelve years his senior. The latter part of Farina's career was affected by the intervention of the Second World War, but he did become the first World Champion when the title was established in 1950. Ascari won it in 1952 and 1953. During this period, Farina won five Grands Prix, Ascari twenty, including the Dutch Grand Prix in 1953 (left). The two are pictured together in the pits at Spa-Francorchamps in 1954 (below). Ascari (right) was not racing that weekend because his car was not ready. He did race at Monaco in 1955 (below, left) and famously crashed this Lancia-Ferrari into the harbour while leading. He swam to safety. Four days later, the great Italian hero was killed during a test session at Monza.

■ FANGIO–MOSS
1955

This was not so much 'Rivalry' as 'Master and Pupil'. Moss, eighteen years the Argentine driver's junior, was only too happy to follow in the wheel tracks of the double World Champion when they raced for Mercedes in 1954 and 1955. Moss would say that watching the maestro from close quarters was the best education a young driver could have. Both drivers were trusted by the legendary Mercedes team manager Alfred Neubauer *(top row, left)* to race each other, the rare occasion when Moss (number 12) beat his team-mate being the 1955 British Grand Prix at Aintree *(bottom, right)*. Moss never did find out if Fangio allowed the young Englishman the honour of winning at home.

Having moved on from being team-mates at Mercedes, Moss and Fangio were up against each other in 1957 when driving for Vanwall and Maserati respectively. The friends and rivals, confer *(top, left)* after a hard afternoon's racing in Italian heat, Moss having beaten Fangio at Pescara. At Monza *(top, right)* Fangio's oversteering 250F leads the Vanwall. In the 1956 Championships *(left)*, Moss congratulates Fangio, who knew he had been fortunate to win the British Grand Prix in his Ferrari after Moss's Maserati had run into trouble in the closing stages.

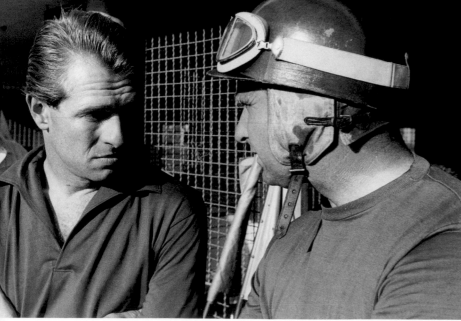

◼ FANGIO–COLLINS
1956

Respect rather than rivalry as Juan Manuel Fangio and Peter Collins *(top row, right)* drove for Ferrari in 1956. Collins won the warm approval not only of Fangio but also Enzo Ferrari at Monza when he stopped of his own accord during the Italian Grand Prix and handed his car over to the Argentine. Fangio's Ferrari had failed and this selfless act not only allowed him to become champion for a fourth time, but it also denied Collins the chance to take a title he was destined never to win. The Englishman (number 2) lines up alongside Fangio's Lancia-Ferrari before the start of the 1956 German Grand Prix *(top row, left)*. Communication between the two was difficult, as Fangio did not speak English and Collins was not fluent in Spanish.

■ COLLINS–FANGIO–HAWTHORN
1958

Mike Hawthorn, an archetypal Englishman with a trademark bow tie, shot to prominence by beating Fangio in an epic wheel-to-wheel battle in the 1953 French Grand Prix at Reims. Even though Fangio usually had the upper hand, they remained rivals for many years, the classic confrontation coming at the Nürburgring in 1957 when Hawthorn and Peter Collins drove for Ferrari. The Britons appeared to have the race under control when Fangio made a pit stop. But the Maserati driver then produced the performance of his life on this long and difficult track, catching and passing them both *(above)*. Collins would be killed on the same circuit a year later, Hawthorn *(above right, right)* losing his life in a road accident after becoming the first British World Champion in 1958. Fangio *(above right, left)* retired in the same year and passed away in 1995, aged eighty-four.

■ MOSS–HAWTHORN
1958

Although great championship rivals in 1958 when Stirling Moss drove for the British Vanwall team and Mike Hawthorn represented Ferrari, the actions of Moss *(above left, right)* during the Portuguese Grand Prix defined sportsmanship at the time. When Hawthorn was threatened with disqualification for going against the race traffic while recovering from a spin on the street circuit, it was Moss who pointed out that his rival had been on the pavement and therefore not on the track at all. Hawthorn kept his six points – and, two races later, beat Moss to the championship by one point despite Moss winning the race in Porto *(above, right)*. One of the fittest and most professional of drivers, Moss was destined to never win the title.

■ PHIL HILL–VON TRIPS
1961

At the start of a new formula for Grand Prix racing in 1961, Ferrari produced a car that would have no equal that year. The 'Sharknose' – so called because of the distinctive twin-nostril air intakes in the nose – won five championship races, allowing Phil Hill of the USA and Wolfgang von Trips to fight for the title. The highly strung but thoughtful American *(above)* had little in common with the cool, aristocratic German who led the championship when it reached the penultimate round in Italy. By finishing third or higher at Monza, von

Trips *(below, right)* would have been crowned champion, but his Ferrari collided with another car and spun off at high speed, killing himself and fifteen spectators. Hill became the first American to win the title and retired from F1 in 1964. He died, aged eighty-one, in California in 2008.

■ SURTEES–HILL–CLARK
1962–64

All three British drivers were in contention when the 1964 championship reached the final round in Mexico. To take the title for the second year in succession, Jim Clark *(right)* needed to win the race, with Graham Hill lower than third and John Surtees lower than second. With Surtees having to finish first or second, Hill was the favourite because he would automatically become champion if the other two did not finish well. There was controversy when Hill, lying third, was hit from behind by Surtees' team-mate Lorenzo Bandini. When Clark's Lotus retired from the lead with engine failure, Surtees *(left)* only had bring his Ferrari home second – which he duly did to become the only man to win World Championships on two wheels and four. Clark and Hill had battled before. As the more senior of the two Britons, Hill had the edge on experience, if not out-and-out speed. Hill, driving for BRM, went head-to-head with Clark for the championship in 1962 *(p.42)*, Hill taking the title when Clark's Lotus ran out of oil during the last race. Clark would have his day in 1963 and 1965, the two then joining forces to make a powerful combination at Lotus in 1967.

Clark brought a sublime skill
to F1 when the quiet Scotsman
struck up a winning relationship
with Colin Chapman, the design
genius behind Lotus. Hill, driving
for BRM, went head-to-head
with Clark for the championship
in 1962 (Clark leads Hill in
Holland, *below*; the pair are
neck-and-neck, centre and left
of the grid in France, *below
right*), Hill's BRM leads Surtees
at Monaco in 1963 *(right)*, the
Ferrari driver going on to win in
Germany *(far right)*.

■ RINDT–STEWART
1969

Rivals, but friends and neighbours in Switzerland, Jackie Stewart and Jochen Rindt engaged in some classic battles, particularly the 1969 British Grand Prix when they swapped the lead many times during an epic contest, victory eventually going to Stewart's Matra-Ford. Stewart won the championship that year, but in 1970 Rindt had the upper hand with his Lotus-Ford. The Austrian was killed during practice for the Italian Grand Prix, but had scored enough points to become Grand Prix racing's only posthumous World Champion. Stewart was devastated, he and his wife Helen *(below left, after Stewart had won the 1969 Dutch GP)* having been close to Jochen and his wife Nina *(below)*. Rindt is best remembered by fans for his spectacular driving style and a fairy-tale victory at Monaco in 1970 after the erstwhile leader, Jack Brabham, had crashed at the final corner when under pressure from the flying Rindt.

■ FITTIPALDI–STEWART
1972–73

Emerson Fittipaldi's *(above right)* meteoric rise in motorsport
continued after winning only his fourth F1 race – the 1970 United
States Grand Prix – and going on to challenge Jackie Stewart
(above left) for the championship two years later. Fittipaldi made
the most of the all-conquering Lotus-Ford to take his first title in
1972, but had a much harder fight with Stewart and his Tyrrell-
Ford during the following season. Fittipaldi won the first two races,
including his home Grand Prix in Brazil, but had to give best to
the Scotsman, a driver he much admired. Stewart, having won his
third championship, retired at the end of 1973.

FITTIPALDI–REGAZZONI
1974

Emerson Fittipaldi moved from Lotus to McLaren *(right)* for 1974 and immediately won the Brazilian Grand Prix. After a challenge from Niki Lauda, Fittipaldi's championship rival would turn out to be Lauda's Ferrari team-mate, Clay Regazzoni *(above)*. The Swiss and the Brazilian were in a shoot-out at the final race in the United States, the two running wheel-to-wheel on the opening lap, with Fittipaldi being forced to put two wheels on the grass at over 160 mph. The McLaren driver did not back off and went on to win his second title. Fittipaldi left McLaren at the end of 1975 to start up an all-Brazilian F1 team, before enjoying much more success by moving into IndyCar racing in the United States and winning the Indianapolis 500 twice. He retired from full-time racing in 1996.

■ HUNT–LAUDA
1976

A rivalry so intense and powerful that it provided the basis of *Rush*, a full-length feature film covering the 1976 season. James Hunt, a dashing young Englishman enjoying his first proper break with a top team, drove for McLaren-Ford *(above, left)*. Lauda, a wily and more seasoned campaigner, having won the title in 1975, raced for Ferrari. A year of protests and controversy would have two key moments: supported by his wife Marlene *(bottom, right)*, Lauda made a remarkable comeback after being badly burned and close to death when his car crashed and caught fire in Germany *(above, right)*. The Austrian then pulled out of the final race in Japan when he considered the streaming-wet conditions too dangerous, allowing Hunt to win the title. Lauda *(overleaf, in middle, talking to Ronnie Peterson)* would go on to win a second championship in 1977 before retiring abruptly, only to return and win a third in 1984. Hunt *(overleaf, left)* retired in 1979, eventually becoming a TV commentator before dying suddenly at the age of 45 in 1993.

■ SCHECKTER–VILLENEUVE
1979

Gilles Villeneuve gave a perfect demonstration of team loyalty in 1979 when he supported Jody Scheckter's successful championship bid, even though the talented French-Canadian was faster at times than the South African. Villeneuve had already been with Ferrari for one season (winning his home Grand Prix in Montreal in 1978) when Scheckter arrived from Wolf as team-leader. They each won three races (above right, Villeneuve at Watkins Glen in the United States) but Villeneuve dutifully remained in Scheckter's wheel tracks (above left) when requested, allowing his team-mate to take the title at Monza, Ferrari's home ground. Scheckter would retire from motorsport at the end of 1980 and go on to start successful businesses in firearms training simulators in the USA and organic farming in England.

■ JONES–PIQUET
1980

Alan Jones did not have a lot of time for South American drivers' style of racing and Nelson Piquet in particular. When they ran head-to-head in the 1980 World Championship, with the impetus regularly swapping between the Brazilian and the Australian, it was bound to end in tears. As if it had been scripted, the pair were side-by-side on the front of the grid for the penultimate race in Canada. Piquet's Brabham-Ford was on pole position, on the inside on the right. When Jones made a slightly better getaway and aimed his Williams-Ford for the right-hand curve immediately after the start, the resulting collision did more damage to the Brabham than the Williams, Piquet having made contact with the concrete wall. When the race was re-started – several cars had been involved in the resulting pile-up – Piquet had to use his back-up machine, which was not as well-prepared as his favoured car. After the Brabham's engine blew up, Jones sailed to the championship. Piquet *(below, right)* sprays the champagne after finishing second in the 1980 British Grand Prix *(below, left)* while Jones holds the winner's trophy.

■ JONES–REUTEMANN
1981

Carlos Reutemann's serious expression *(far right)* sums up the relationship with Alan Jones when the Argentine driver was the Australian's team-mate at Williams in 1981. As reigning World Champion and having enjoyed a comfortable history with the team, Jones was the de facto number-one driver and was supposed to be allowed to win the Brazilian Grand Prix early in the year. When Reutemann ignored team orders and took the victory, an icy atmosphere set in for the remainder of the season. Reutemann, through first-class performances such as his win in Belgium *(below, leading Piquet's Brabham)*, got himself into the lead of the championship, but lost his chance at the final race in Las Vegas after starting from pole and finishing out of the points. A commanding win for Jones *(right)* in the same race exacerbated Reutemann's disappointment as much as it quietly pleased his team-mate.

■ PROST–ARNOUX
1982

Despite fielding a competitive car, Renault's hopes of winning the championship for the first time in 1982 were compromised by the disorderly behaviour of René Arnoux *(above)*. The Frenchman agreed to allow Alain Prost *(right)* to win their home Grand Prix because his fellow-countryman had a better chance of taking the title thanks to scoring more points thus far. When Arnoux took an early lead, Prost was happy to conserve his car and tyres, knowing he would be allowed to take command later in the race. But Arnoux never let up and ignored pit signals reminding him of the agreement. Prost's fury multiplied when the Renault management failed to tell the world what had been agreed, giving the false impression that Prost was being a bad loser when he said he could have won the race had he known from the outset that he was racing his team-mate. Renault did not win the championship and it took several years before the French drivers spoke amicably again.

■ PIRONI–VILLENEUVE
1982

The story of a short but bitter rivalry with a tragic conclusion. Gilles Villeneuve had become a stalwart at Ferrari when Didier Pironi joined the Italian team in 1982. Villeneuve had no need of team orders, but it seemed a good idea when the potentially fragile Ferraris had no opposition to speak of in the San Marino Grand Prix. Rather than race each other to destruction, it was agreed that whoever was in front in the early going would be allowed to stay there until the finish. When Pironi overtook Villeneuve and led during the closing stages *(right)*, Villeneuve assumed it was for show, to keep the Ferrari fans amused. But rather than put on an act, Pironi was serious about winning and stayed out of Villeneuve's reach. The French-Canadian was livid, spoke of Pironi's duplicity and vowed never to speak to the Frenchman again. It was a threat with a terrible resonance. Two weeks later, while trying to better Pironi's qualifying time for the Belgian Grand Prix *(below)*, Villeneuve collided with a slower car that had inadvertently moved into his path. Villeneuve died of injuries received when thrown from the cockpit of the cavorting Ferrari.

■ PIQUET–PROST
1983

The story of 1983 was not so much that Nelson Piquet *(right)* had won the World Championship, but that Alain Prost had lost it. Prost and Renault *(above)* had been the favourites but, not for the first time, their chances had been frittered away as they came under increasing threat from Piquet and Brabham-BMW. Prost won four races to Piquet's three, the pair colliding in Holland after Prost had misjudged an overtaking move, all of which turned up the pressure another notch. Going into the final race in South Africa, Prost led by two points. Believing they were about to witness the crowning of their first World Champion, the French media descended on Kyalami in their droves – only to be stunned when the Renault, never in the hunt, broke down. Prost was heavily criticised by the French reporters, the majority of whom did not understand how F1 worked. He left Renault almost immediately and joined McLaren. Piquet, with a second title under his belt, stayed with Brabham before moving on to Williams.

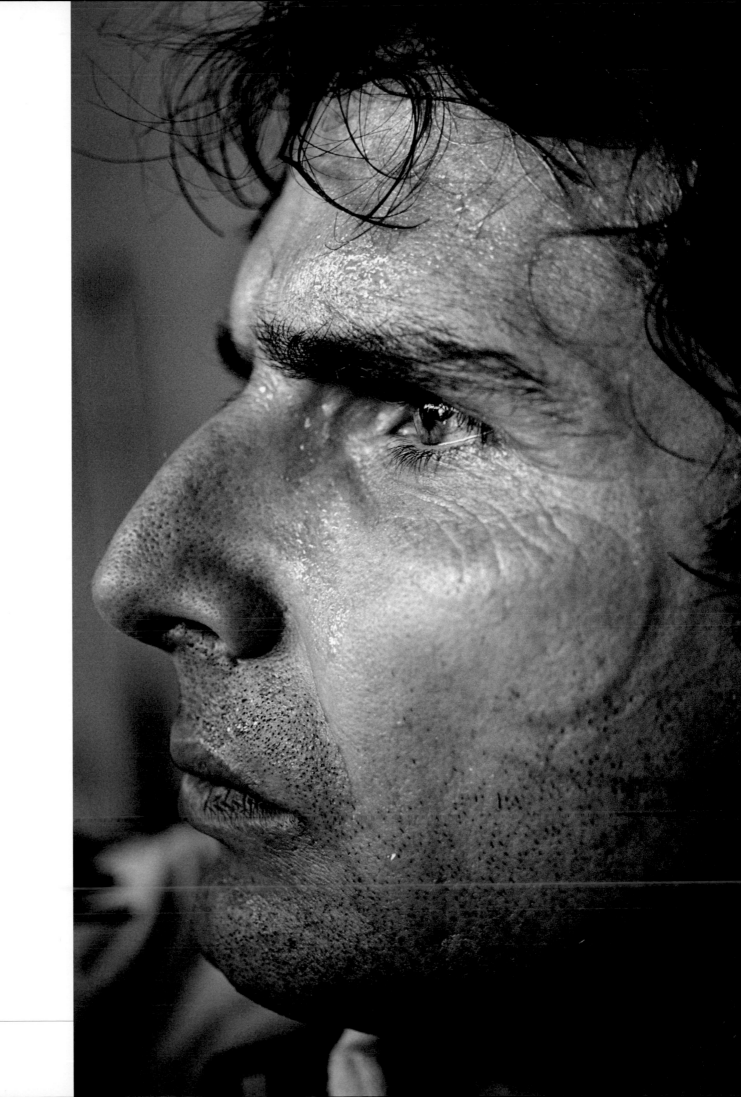

■ PROST–LAUDA
1984

Finding themselves with the best car – the McLaren-TAG Turbo – Alain Prost and Niki Lauda were free to race each other for the title. It would turn out to be the closest finish in the history of the championship, Lauda *(above left, on the right)* beating Prost by half a point (the anomaly of the half-point created by the Monaco Grand Prix having been stopped early because of heavy rain and half-points awarded, Prost receiving 4.5 points instead of nine for winning). Lauda was in the twilight of a distinguished F1 career but no less canny for that. Realising that his young team-mate was faster, Lauda used his guile and experience to focus on collecting points rather than being fastest all the time. Each driver had great respect for the other, making it one of the most productive, amicable and yet seriously competitive partnerships in the history of the F1 championship. Prost, as Lauda predicted, went on to win four world titles, while the Austrian retired for a second time at the end of the following year.

■ MANSELL–SENNA
1985–89

The enmity between Nigel Mansell and Ayrton Senna took hold in 1985 and would run in two phases into the 1990s. It started when both drivers, united only by an iron will to win, scored maiden wins in 1985, the year Senna replaced Mansell in the John Player Special Lotus *(right)*. Mansell was much more at home with Williams-Honda and the raging impulse to beat each other continued into 1987, reaching its most dramatic peak in Belgium when the pair collided, Mansell later attempting to throttle his rival in the Lotus garage. Even after Senna *(below)* switched to McLaren-Honda and Mansell to Ferrari, the animosity continued when they collided yet again during the 1989 Portuguese Grand Prix, as Mansell tried an ambitious move that added fuel to a fire started when he ignored a black flag signalling him to stop for an earlier indiscretion. It fostered a deep-seated antagonism that would resume a few years later.

■ MANSELL–PIQUET
1986–87

Sharing the competitiveness of the Williams-Honda in 1986 and 1987, Nigel Mansell and Nelson Piquet may have been in the same team but were never on the same side. The mutual antipathy was evident from the outset as the Brazilian poked fun at his very British counterpart. In the absence of team orders, it was every man for himself – as was proved in Hungary (*opposite, top, left*) when Piquet found a performance tweak for his car that he didn't share with his team-mate. Mansell (*opposite, bottom, right*) found out about it when lapped by Piquet's winning car. Mansell gained more impressive high ground in 1987 when, in a straight fight, he beat Piquet by pulling off a brave overtaking move to win the British Grand Prix (*above*). Piquet (*opposite, top, right*) had the last laugh by winning the championship that year, unlike 1986, when the pair had run neck-and-neck and taken enough points off each other to allow Alain Prost to slip through and take the championship at the final race.

■ SENNA–PROST
1988–90

The most infamous rivalry of them all. Ayrton Senna *(bottom row, middle)* joined McLaren-Honda in 1988 knowing that Alain Prost *(middle row, centre)*, with the team since 1984, was considered to be the best driver of the era. Senna's intense desire to prove himself by beating the Frenchman began to surface in Portugal near the end of 1988 when he eased Prost towards the pit wall at 175mph. It really got going the following year when a row blew up after Senna had broken a private agreement with Prost and taken victory in the San Marino Grand Prix. When the championship boiled down to these two drivers, the inevitable collision took place at the penultimate race as they fought for the lead, the title going to Prost. Infuriated over what he perceived to be unjust treatment, Senna took the law into his own hands at the same race a year later and drove Prost, now with Ferrari *(top row, right)* off the road, winning the championship in the process. They battled less often in 1993 when Prost switched to Williams-Renault *(overleaf),* and there would be an unexpected and complete rapprochement when Prost retired at the end of that year, six months before Senna was killed at Imola.

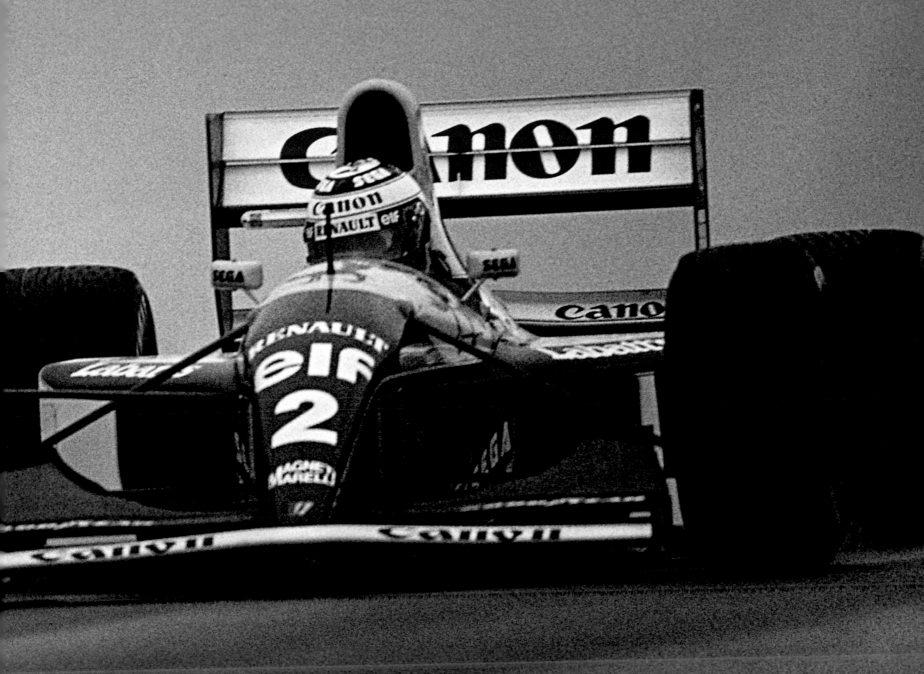

■ MANSELL–SENNA
1991–92

The rivalry between the Brazilian and the Englishman picked up again in 1991 when Mansell once more had a very competitive car at his disposal. With maturity and experience came a grudging respect that saw Mansell give Senna a lift on his victorious Williams-Renault after Senna's McLaren-Honda had broken down during the 1991 British Grand Prix. The sight of the pair running within inches of each other – and without contact – at 190 mph while fighting for the lead in Barcelona later that year remains one of the sport's most iconic images. Mansell would win the world crown in 1992, but not before Senna had used his guile to win in Monaco *(right)* and sucker Mansell into a crash as they fought for position during the Canadian Grand Prix. Mansell would switch to IndyCar racing in 1993, making a brief return to F1 in 1994 and in 1995 after Senna's fatal accident in the San Marino Grand Prix.

■ SCHUMACHER–HILL
1994–95

When Ayrton Senna was killed at Imola in May 1994, Damon Hill *(below and bottom row, left and right)* found himself elevated to team leader at Williams-Renault – and straight into conflict with Benetton's Michael Schumacher *(second row)*. The German would become Hill's nemesis in a championship battle that saw Hill score classy wins (particularly in Japan) and would run until the last race when they collided while disputing the lead of the Australian

Grand Prix. Both were out but the title went to Schumacher. The following year, Hill was consistently beaten (they collided twice more) as Schumacher won his second championship, but the Englishman regrouped in 1996 to take the title after Schumacher had switched to the uncompetitive Ferrari team. They never did become the best of friends, not even after Hill retired in 1999 following stints with Arrows and Jordan.

■ SCHUMACHER–VILLENEUVE
1997

After a shaky start as Ferrari reorganised in 1996, the combination of the Italian team and Schumacher *(above, and below left)* began to come good the following year and to lock into battle with the Williams-Renault of Jacques Villeneuve. As in 1994, the championship went down to the wire, but this time Schumacher lost out following another collision with his rival in the last race. When Villeneuve *(above right, bottom right)* tried to overtake during the European Grand Prix at Jerez in Spain, the French-Canadian (son of Gilles Villeneuve) found the Ferrari turning in on him. The deliberate move by Schumacher raised questions about the part he had played in Hill's demise three years before and also earned a reprimand, Schumacher being stripped of his 1997 championship points. Villeneuve would spend another eight seasons in F1, but would never enjoy the same level of competitiveness.

◼ SCHUMACHER–HAKKINEN
1998–2000

Ferrari's bid to win the championship with Schumacher for the first time since Jody Scheckter in 1979 was heavily compromised by the energetic presence of Mika Hakkinen and McLaren-Mercedes *(above)*, the Finn edging out his rivals by narrow margins in 1998 and 1999. By and large, the contest was clean. Schumacher would learn the hard way that his rival was not a driver to be messed with when, in a pass of spine-tingling commitment and bravery at Spa-Francorchamps, Hakkinen went one side of a backmarker while Schumacher went the other as they braked from 200mph for the following corner. The move gave Hakkinen the lead; fair reward he felt for having had Schumacher cut in front of him at the same spot a lap earlier. This was in 2000, the year Schumacher and Ferrari finally became champions. Hakkinen would quit F1 at the end of the following year.

(Opposite, clockwise from top left)
In 1998, Schumacher celebrates
victory at Monza, heads for
another win at a wet Silverstone
and points the Ferrari towards
a podium finish in Austria.
(Above) Schumacher prepares to
evacuate the cockpit in Germany.

■ IRVINE–HAKKINEN
1999

Marked out to play a supporting role to his Ferrari team-mate, Eddie Irvine *(below right)* was thrust into the championship equation halfway through the 1999 season when Schumacher crashed and broke a leg during the British Grand Prix. When the German made a return for the last two races, roles were reversed as he did what he could to assist Irvine's fight with McLaren's Mika Hakkinen *(below left)*. The Ulsterman eased into the reckoning by winning the penultimate round in Malaysia, with Schumacher demoting Hakkinen to third. But, in the final race in Japan, Irvine was sidelined with a mysterious handling problem, allowing Hakkinen to win both the race and the title. Irvine would never come so close again during three seasons with Jaguar before retiring at the end of 2002.

■ ALONSO–SCHUMACHER
2006

Fernando Alonso (*above*) and Michael Schumacher dominated the 2006 World Championship, each winning seven races for Renault and Ferrari respectively. A very strong first half of the season kept Alonso ahead but Schumacher fought back, victory in China putting the German in front in the title race for the first time with two races to go. A first and a second in Japan and Brazil were enough to make Alonso the youngest driver to win back to back World Championships. Schumacher would quit F1 at the end of the season, making a return with Mercedes in 2010 but showing none of the dominance that had effectively been ended by Alonso's two strong seasons.

■ HAMILTON–ALONSO
2007

Fernando Alonso joined McLaren-Mercedes for 2007 to lead Lewis Hamilton in his first F1 season. It was a dream team that turned into a nightmare thanks to the young Englishman's precocious performances and Alonso's increasing paranoia when, in his view, Hamilton's speed should have been kept in check by McLaren management. Alonso led the championship after winning the second race in Malaysia and the fifth in Monaco, but then had to give best to his team-mate as Hamilton *(bottom, right)* won

two races and led the title race all the way to the final round – by which time the relationship had deteriorated to the point where Alonso, despite winning in Italy *(below)*, had become a disgruntled loose cannon. Added to which, McLaren had to deal with the damage created by allegations of spying by Ferrari, whose driver, Kimi Räikkönen, lifted the championship at the final race, having led only briefly early on. Alonso left immediately, while Hamilton stayed on for another five years.

■ HAMILTON–MASSA
2008

In one of the greatest cliff-hangers in the history of the World Championship, Lewis Hamilton *(near right, and far right columns)* won the title at the last corner of the last race in Brazil. For ten seconds, Felipe Massa *(middle column)*, having won his home race, thought he was champion, until Hamilton made up one crucial position a quarter of a mile from the finish. It summed up a hugely dramatic season as Massa led the title chase halfway through before Hamilton began a run of high point-scoring, only to be taken out by a collision with Massa three races from the end. Massa had his share of bad luck while leading in Singapore only to be waved away from a pit stop with the fuel line still attached. It would be the closest Massa has yet come to winning the title; he survived a potentially fatal injury in 2009 and was still racing in F1 in 2016.

■ VETTEL-WEBBER
2010–13

Sebastian Vettel *(above)* won four championships in succession between 2010 and 2013, the early years in particular being enlivened by an increasingly tense battle with his Red Bull team-mate, Mark Webber *(opposite top, left)*. There was little love lost between the Australian and Vettel, particularly in 2010 when the pair collided as the German tried to take the lead in Turkey. Vettel had become edgy after Webber's victories in the previous two races, including the difficult and prestigious Monaco Grand Prix. Webber was ahead of Vettel on points going into the final race in Abu Dhabi but pole position for Vettel and a clean race gave him the title as Webber became bogged down in traffic. Webber would never get a better opportunity during his remaining three years in F1 before switching to become World Endurance Champion in 2015.

■ HAMILTON–ROSBERG
2014–16

Headline-grabbing rivalry of recent years as Lewis Hamilton (*below, far left*) made the move from McLaren to join Nico Rosberg (*below, left*) at Mercedes for 2014. Hamilton knew the German well, the pair having grown up together through karting and the junior formulae. Their lap times in the dominant Mercedes were frequently separated by fractions of a second – the click of a finger. But when it came to the ruthless bare-knuckle fight needed to succeed in such a situation, Hamilton would usually come out on top. Frustrated by his team-mate's aggression, Rosberg's attempt at resisting a pass in Belgium resulted in Hamilton's left-rear tyre being punctured – and Rosberg being further upset by the criticism that came his way. Hamilton won the title at the final race of 2014 and, emboldened by his second championship, drove better than ever and took a third before the end of the 2015 season. But not before more controversy as he eased Rosberg off the road in the US Grand Prix. Released from the pressure of the championship, Rosberg then moved onto a higher plane – with Hamilton relaxing a little – and won the final three races in truly dominant style, thus setting the scene for 2016, when Rosberg (*overleaf*) finally clinched the title in Abu Dhabi.

■ RICCIARDO–VERSTAPPEN
2016

Max Verstappen's rise to stardom accelerated halfway through 2016 when the Dutch teenager was promoted from Toro Rosso to Red Bull – and promptly won his first Grand Prix in Spain, becoming the youngest-ever driver to do so at the age of eighteen (*top and bottom, right*). This presented an immediate challenge to Daniel Ricciardo (*above*) – a highly promising young driver himself – who responded magnificently to his new team-mate's insouciance. The pair produced an enthralling and clean wheel-to-wheel contest when fighting for the lead of the Malaysian Grand Prix, victory going to Ricciardo. But these were early days in the relationship as Verstappen found his feet. It was widely anticipated that, should the Red Bull pair be in the running for further wins, or the championship, the partnership would become as testy as any rivalry between two highly-talented young chargers, neither of whom was prepared to back down.

TEAMS AND CARS

FOR SPEED

Motorsport fans are intensely loyal. But while many attach their allegiance to a particular driver, others remain devoted to a single team. The cult of family and passion generated by an established team will often outweigh dedication to the star performer. The driver is transient; enjoying his moment before either moving on or retiring. The team will be there, if not forever, then for quite some time. That, at least, is the plan. A glance at the historical register of F1 teams, however, shows just how difficult that can be.

Since the start of the F1 World Championship in 1950, more than sixty-five teams have taken part. Only one – Ferrari – has stayed the course. Of the current teams, McLaren has been in F1 since 1966; Williams, in various guises, since 1973. The rest vary from twenty-five years to novice, as demonstrated by the Haas team entering F1 in 2016.

The American name has been added to a list that actually began long before the World Championship was invented sixty-six years ago. In fact, the origins of the sport demonstrate the importance of machine over man, as the first motor races at the turn of the twentieth century allowed one motor manufacturer to show its superiority over another. The race from Paris to Rouen in 1894 was all about Peugeot against Panhard and other car companies rather than the skill of the drivers coping with these spindly machines on rutted and dusty roads.

The trend would continue until the Second World War interrupted dramatic battles between Auto Union and Mercedes-Benz who fought for supremacy, not just in Germany but internationally. When sport resumed in the mid-1940s, the value of racing continued to be of interest to car companies, the Italians joining the fray with teams from Maserati, Alfa Romeo and, significantly, Ferrari.

Enzo Ferrari may have started out as a driver, but he was astute enough to see racing as a means of advertising his exotic road-going sports cars, the sale of which funded his motor racing. Ferrari was living for the moment and, much as he would have enjoyed the thought, it's a fair bet he did not dream of his racing team being viewed as a motorsport icon several decades later.

He did, however, live through an era of change, one that would accelerate even more dramatically in the years following his death at the age of ninety in 1988. Before then, however, Ferrari had done more than any other entrant to perpetuate the dramatic image and raison d'être of a team pursuing motor racing at the highest level.

The undeniable fact is that much of the melodrama was created by the Italian autocrat setting his drivers against each other at a time when safety was not a priority and fatalities were common. In the view of Enzo Ferrari, the best drivers may have been brilliant but they had to be regarded as expendable. Indeed, in his openly expressed opinion, they were lucky to be racing for Ferrari.

There is a certain amount of truth in the fact that a top driver is impotent without a fast and reliable car but, equally, many promising careers could be wrecked by a top team enduring a single season of uncompetitiveness. In this cyclical business, Ferrari had several of those, even though his personal desire for speed remained undiminished. But when his crafty gamesmanship blended with clever technology, Ferrari's unstoppable force would add another chapter to the growing legend.

His handling of a change of engine formula for the 1961 season was a perfect example of adroit political subterfuge. While the British teams bemoaned the new formula, threatening boycotts and talking of lobbying for a more attractive alternative, Enzo Ferrari agreed with them. But all the while, his team was beavering away at being fully prepared for the latest regulations as soon as the season started. While the British wrung their hands and cried unfair, Ferrari dominated the championship. When the opposition caught up in 1962, the Ferrari team was nowhere. Such is the roller-coaster intrigue of F1.

Being one step ahead has always been the yardstick. When the formula changed again in 1966, Jack Brabham was prepared. Instead of investing in complex plans for the latest engines, the wily Australian developed a unit based on a tried and trusted V8 from America. It may not have been the most advanced engine ever seen in F1 but it was reliable – and ready. His cars won the championship for two successive seasons.

As the years went by and technology advanced rapidly, Colin Chapman tapped into it better than most. The mercurial genius dreamed up the wedge-shaped Lotus 72 that would dominate the scene in the early 1970s. Not satisfied with that, Chapman took a huge step forward when he invented so-called 'ground effect', a development that effectively sucked the car to the track and allowed Mario Andretti to destroy the opposition in 1978.

In between, there had been a bad patch for Lotus – as would happen to Williams after their cars had been a major force throughout the early 1980s. Williams, in turn,

Top left
Jim Clark in the Lotus 49 at Monza in 1967.

Top right
Clark and Colin Chapman in the pits at Zandvoort in 1965.

Bottom left
The heavy Maserati V12 in the back of John Surtees's Cooper at Monza in 1966.

Bottom Right
Dan Gurney contemplates the back of his Eagle-Weslake at Monaco in 1968.

Overleaf
Michele Alboreto was one of many Italians to carry the weight of national expectation as a Ferrari driver.

Top left
Brabham's Nelson Piquet prepares for the start at Zolder in 1982.

Top right
James Hunt in the Hesketh 308 in the 1974 German Grand Prix.

Left
Michael Schumacher and Ferrari at Imola in 2000.

were usurped by McLaren, as the team from Surrey mated a purpose-built engine from Porsche with an equally competitive chassis made from carbon fibre, a material that McLaren had used to revolutionise F1 not long before. But unlike its rivals, McLaren kept the ball rolling into the 1990s with a timely switch to Honda engines and an equally powerful driving pairing of Ayrton Senna and Alain Prost.

And so it continued, the impetus shifting back to Williams, then on to the newly formed Benetton team, back to McLaren (now with Mercedes engines), followed by a long run for Michael Schumacher and the ever-present red cars from Ferrari at the start of the 2000s. A brief period for Renault led to a four-year domination by Red Bull until another change of engine formula for 2014 saw Mercedes – now running their own team instead of just supplying engines – being better prepared than most.

It has been a dictum of motor racing that Mercedes understood through past experience. In 1954, the German team had returned to F1 and steamrollered the opposition from the word go with their superior silver machines. It was eloquent proof that the desire for speed has never changed, no matter the colour of the car or who may be driving it – as any F1 fan will confirm.

■ McLAREN

Founded by Bruce McLaren *(right)* in 1963, the early days of McLaren Racing are encapsulated by the images above. The two cars parked randomly *(above)* with drivers Denny Hulme *(left)* and McLaren sitting on the front wheels, casually preparing for a photo call in the pit lane at Jarama, sum up the relaxed small-team atmosphere in 1968. As does the shot *(top right)* of Hulme sprawled across the front of the car driven by his boss and Kiwi mate, Bruce. The cars were originally sprayed orange when Gulf represented the leading sponsor, prior to the arrival of Marlboro in the late 1970s. Alain Prost, in the foreground *(bottom right, middle)*, waits in the pit lane at Monza in 1985, the way barred by the JPS Lotus of Ayrton Senna before the Brazilian joined Prost at McLaren. The pair would win championships for McLaren before the arrival of Mika Häkkinen *(p.126)* and Lewis Hamilton *(p.127)*.

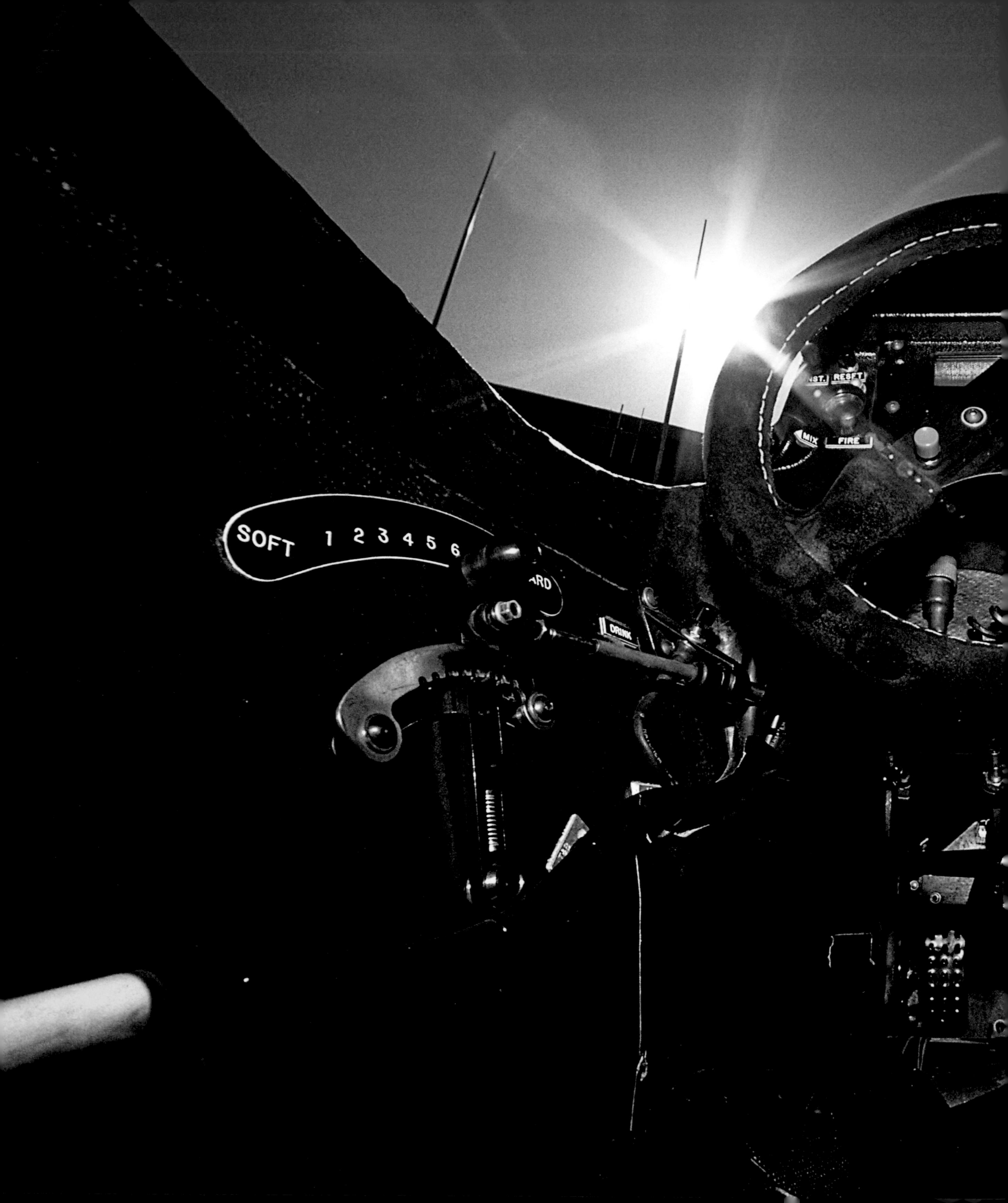
SOFT 1 2 3 4 5 6
RESET
MIX
FIRE
DRINK

Mika Hakkinen   Lewis Hamilton

Fernando Alonso

■ FERRARI

The images on the following pages illustrate the many shapes but consistently charismatic red of Ferrari through the decades, as befits the longest-serving team in F1. From the front-engine machines of the 1950s *(Phil Hill above, left)* to the chisel-nose profile of cars three decades later *(above, right)*, all have carried the famous Prancing Horse insignia that represents the most famous name in motorsport. The story of this great team abounds with personalities, starting with Enzo Ferrari himself *(p.130 bottom, far left, talking to Phil Hill)* and moving through drivers such as Froilán González, winner of Ferrari's first championship Grand Prix *(top, left)* to Giuseppi Farina *(top, centre)*, John Surtees *(bottom, far right)* and Mike Hawthorn *(chasing the Vanwall of Tony Brooks at the Nürburgring in 1958, centre)* with brilliant engineers including a pensive Mauro Forghieri, seated in the 1963 Ferrari at Silverstone *(top and centre, right)*.

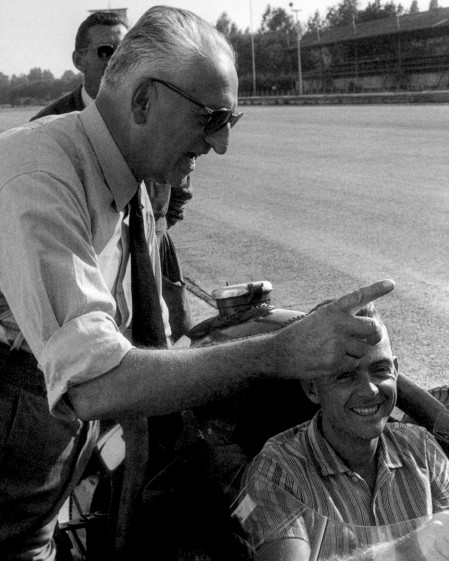

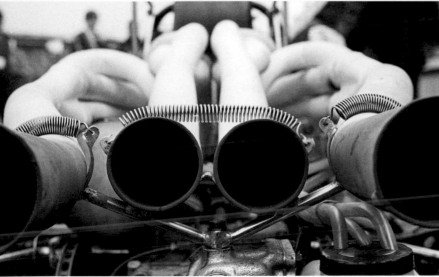

Little can match the imposing sight of five Lancia-Ferraris, waiting for the start of practice at Monza in 1956.

Niki Lauda and Carlos
Reutemann: Monza 1977.

Patrick Tambay : Detroit 1983.

Mechanics at work: Estoril 1988
(top) and Interlagos 1991.

Kimi Raikkonen : Silverstone 2007.

Gerhard Berger : Argentina 1995.

Rubens Barrichello: Imola 2004.

Sebastian Vettel racing for
Ferrari in Monaco 2016.

Overleaf
Gilles Villeneuve in typical
power-sliding pose with his
Ferrari during the 1980 French
Grand Prix at Paul Ricard.

Michael Schumacher at Magny-Cours in France after one of his seventy-two wins for the team.

■ MATRA

The aerospace company was in the vanguard of a French invasion of F1 in the late 1960s. Using aero industry techniques, Matra built chassis notable for their stiffness and precise handling. The attack on F1 was two-pronged. A works car, in the hands of Jean-Pierre Beltoise and powered by a glorious-sounding V12 engine, made its debut at Monaco *(above)* in 1968. Matra's principal success came with chassis – powered by a Ford V8 – farmed out to the British Tyrrell team and their driver, Jackie Stewart. The Scotsman scored an outstanding victory with the Matra-Ford MS10 in the 1968 German Grand Prix run in appalling conditions *(above, right)* and went on to win the championship for Tyrrell-Matra the following year with the MS80 *(right)*. That would be the high point of Matra's success. They lost the association with Tyrrell thanks to an insistence on running their own car and V12 engine, before withdrawing from F1 at the end of 1972.

■ JORDAN

This was a small but colourful team that arrived in F1 in 1991 after the owner, Eddie Jordan, had won championships in the junior ranks. After almost winning a Grand Prix during their first season, Jordan finished a creditable fifth in the championship. Sometimes handicapped by switching engine supplier in a bid to find the best deal, it would take Jordan until 1998 to win their first Grand Prix, with two more the following year bringing the British-based team within striking distance of the title. It was a gradual downhill decline from there until the team was sold in 2005 but, throughout, Jordan maintained a lively presence by giving full value to sponsors, principally the tobacco company Benson and Hedges *(left, Martin Brundle at the wheel of the gold-painted Jordan-Peugeot in 1996)*. Jordan is likely to remain one of the last of the small teams ever to win a Grand Prix.

■ RENAULT

The French automotive giant has been in F1 in many guises over four decades. Initially as a pioneer of turbocharged engines in their own car in 1977, Renault won Grands Prix but narrowly missed out on championships, before withdrawing as a team to act as engine supplier for others. They returned in 2002 to take over Benetton and went on to score great success in 2005 and 2006 when Fernando Alonso *(left)* won back-to-back championships. Then there followed a decline not helped by the global financial recession and a reputation tarnished by allegations of race fixing by team management in the 2008 Singapore Grand Prix. Renault focussed solely on engine supply once more from 2012, before making a return as an entrant by taking over their former team for 2016.

■ TYRRELL

Arguably the most successful new arrival of any small manufacturer, Ken Tyrrell was forced to build his own car in 1970 when other car makers were reluctant to supply a chassis to the reigning champion. Built in a wood yard in Surrey, the first Tyrrell-Ford led its debut Grand Prix at the end of 1970 and went on to provide the basis for Jackie Stewart's second championship the following year. With continuous backing from Elf, Stewart and Tyrrell-Ford dominated again in 1973 *(above)*. François Cevert *(far left, left)* was due to take over from Stewart as number one when the Scotsman retired at the end of the year, but the Frenchman was killed during practice for the final race at Watkins Glen in the USA. Tyrrell produced a revolutionary six-wheel car *(p.149)* and went on to win a few more Grand Prixs with Jody Scheckter and Patrick Depailler *(left)* but it was to mark the start of a slow and, at times, painful decline for this very British team before being bought by British American Tobacco in 1998.

Left
Patrick Depailler

Above
Tyrrell produced a revolutionary six-wheel car.

■ BRM

Founded in 1945-46, initially as a cooperative industrial Grand Prix car venture, British Racing Motors was a bold enterprise, manufacturing its own chassis, engine and gearbox. At its peak in the 1960s, BRM was a major force in F1, despite winning just one driver's title with Graham Hill in 1962. The Englishman (pictured, after his first-ever GP win at Zandvoort in 1962) was a stalwart of a team that slowly began to lose its way after Hill departed in 1967. Runner-up in the Constructors' Championship for a fourth time in 1971, BRM scored their seventeenth and final victory with Jean-Pierre Beltoise in a wet Monaco Grand Prix in 1972. The British team struggled on in different guises until finally closing its doors in the early 1980s after competing in 197 championship Grands Prix.

■ LOTUS

Lotus is second only to Ferrari as an iconic name thanks to entering F1 in 1958 and winning several championships, notably with Jim Clark in the 1960s. The quiet Scot *(bottom, middle)* made the most of the pioneering cars designed by Colin Chapman *(peaked cap, top left)*, one of the outstanding combinations being Clark and the Lotus-Ford 49 *(above, right)*. Clark was killed in 1968 before he could make full use of this car and carry on great battles with his fellow countryman, Jackie Stewart *(with Clark, right)*. Chapman went on to win more titles with Jochen Rindt *(p.154)* and Emerson Fittipaldi *(p.155)* after breaking further new ground with the Lotus-Ford 72 *(p.156; Ronnie Peterson at Monaco in 1973)*. When Chapman died suddenly in 1982, the team lost momentum briefly and failed to give Elio de Angelis *(p.157)* the chance he deserved. The arrival of Ayrton Senna in 1985 helped regain the impetus, as Lotus won more Grands Prix and were in the running for the title. The decline was sudden in the early 1990s, the famous name being bought and used by other teams to no lasting effect.

Left
Jochen Rindt

Below
Jochen Rindt with Colin Chapman

Right
Emerson Fittipaldi

Far right
Emerson Fittipaldi with Colin Chapman

Below right
Emerson Fittipaldi

Ronnie Peterson with the Lotus
72 at Monaco in 1973.

Elio de Angelis

■ EAGLE

The American Dan Gurney *(right)* created one of the most beautiful cars in F1 when he built the Eagle, which he then took to victory in the 1967 Belgian Grand Prix *(above)*. Powered by a Weslake V12 engine, this car, entered by All American Racers (AAR), would be the highlight of the team's relatively brief association with F1. Initially intending to compete in the Indianapolis 500 as well as F1, Gurney saw a change of engine formula in 1966 as an advantageous moment. A smart engineer as well as a world-class driver, Gurney used a stopgap 4-cylinder Climax engine while waiting for the V12 to be completed by Weslake in Sussex, England. The combination won the non-championship Race of Champions at Brands Hatch in March 1967 before encountering various difficulties in subsequent Grands Prix. It all came good in Belgium, the victory at Spa-Francorchamps being the zenith of Gurney's efforts with the Eagle before AAR bowed out of F1 in 1969.

■ LIGIER

The French team was founded by Guy Ligier, a former international rugby player who used money made in the construction business to fund his passion for motorsport. A former private entrant and driver in F1, Ligier created a team to successfully race sports cars before moving into Grand Prix racing in 1976. Over the next twenty years, Ligier would use a succession of engines, ranging from Matra and Renault to Lamborghini. His greatest success came with Ford-V8-powered cars in 1979 when victories with the JS11 in South America put Ligier at the forefront, only to lose the championship because the drivers, Jacques Laffite *(left)* and Patrick Depailler, had joint number one status and took points off each other. Laffite *(above, in the 1982 Swiss Grand Prix at Dijon)* remained a stalwart of the team over nine seasons and scored Ligier's maiden victory with a Matra-powered JS7 in the 1977 Swedish Grand Prix. Ligier claimed nine Grands Prix wins in total, the last being an unexpected victory in changeable conditions at Monaco in 1996. Guy Ligier sold the team at the end of the year.

■ JAGUAR

The Ford Motor Company brought the Jaguar name into F1 in 2000 by buying Stewart Grand Prix, a team founded three years earlier by former champion, Sir Jackie Stewart. Whereas Stewart had won a Grand Prix during their brief existence, Jaguar would fail thanks to dysfunctional management during the course of eighty-five Grands Prix, the highlights being third places for Eddie Irvine *(above right)* in Monaco in 2001 and in Italy the following year. Mark Webber replaced Irvine *(above, storming away from a pit stop in Spain in 2001)* for the final two seasons, by which time new management had begun to bring improvements – but no results worth speaking of for the Ford-powered car. Having ventured into F1 to promote the premium Jaguar brand, Ford did not feel the expenditure was justified and called a halt at the end of 2004.

■ RED BULL

The Austrian energy drinks company bought the Jaguar F1 team in November 2004 and renamed it Red Bull Racing (RBR). Investment began to pay off in the first year when RBR won more championship points than Jaguar had managed in the previous two seasons. A major turning point came at the end of the year with the hiring of Adrian Newey as technical chief and, for 2009, the promotion of Sebastian Vettel from Toro Rosso, effectively a junior team for RBR. The combination took its maiden win in China, a prelude to Vettel scoring four successive world titles between 2010 and 2013, ending Ferrari's dominance *(above left, Vettel shakes hands with Fernando Alonso after the 2013 Singapore Grand Prix)*. Along the way, Vettel also faced strong opposition from his team-mate, Mark Webber *(above, far left)*. Having briefly used Ford and Ferrari engines in the early years, RBR's success had come through close ties with Renault, but the relationship came under strain following the engine manufacturer's failure to meet the demands of new and complex technical regulations for 2014. For the first time in six years, Red Bull failed to win a race in 2015 but won twice the following year.

■ COOPER

Cooper is best remembered for pioneering work in the late 1950s when the British team set the trend by moving the engine from the front to the rear of the car. Jack Brabham won successive championships in 1959 and 1960. The Australian is pictured (above, right) with Bruce McLaren, who also won for Cooper in 1959 before starting his own eponymous team. As others caught up with Cooper's technical advances, success became sporadic. Despite the sometimes spectacular efforts of Jochen Rindt (near left) with the hefty Maserati-powered car, it was Pedro Rodriguez (far left) who scored Cooper's last win in the 1967 South African Grand Prix. After sixteen wins, Cooper withdrew from Grand Prix racing in 1969.

■ MASERATI

Maserati competed in Grand Prix racing in the 1940s and 50s. The Italian firm produced three classic Grand Prix cars, the most famous – and certainly most enjoyed by its drivers – being the 250F. Luigi Musso prepares to leave the pits at Spa in 1955 *(above)* while Juan Manuel Fangio *(top right, and right)* used this sleek front-engine classic to win the last of his five world titles in 1957, shortly before financial difficulties forced Maserati to close its racing team. Privateers continued to campaign the 250F and Maserati had a presence in F1 thanks to supplying engines to the Cooper team in 1966 and 1967. Maserati competed in sixty-eight championship Grands Prix and won nine of them.

■ BRABHAM

Jack Brabham *(above, and near right)* became the first man to win a race and then a World Championship driving a car bearing his name. Having won championships with Cooper, Brabham left to build and race his own cars in 1962 and really came into his own in 1966 when a new formula was introduced. Better prepared than most, Brabham won four races to take the title, his team-mate Denny Hulme *(far right)* winning the championship the following year. Not long after Brabham retired at the end of 1970, his team was bought by Bernie Ecclestone, who kept the name and went on to win races and championships in the early 1980s. Along the way, the team caused uproar during 1978 when Niki Lauda won the Swedish Grand Prix *(above, right)* with a car fitted at the rear with a huge fan that helped suck the car to the ground. Victory in the 1985 French Grand Prix would be the last for Brabham before the team changed hands and went into rapid decline.

■ WILLIAMS

This is a British team much admired and respected, largely through the dogged determination and relentless efforts of its founder, Sir Frank Williams. Having lived hand-to-mouth in the early 1970s, Williams turned a corner in 1977 when he won sponsorship from the Middle East. He rebuilt his team into a race winner, the first being the British Grand Prix in 1979, one year before Williams' Alan Jones became World Champion, the team also winning the constructors' title. Further titles followed with Keke Rosberg in 1982 and Damon Hill in 1996 *(p.174)*. Many top drivers have passed through the team, including David Coulthard and Juan Pablo Montoya. But perhaps the best remembered for more unfortunate reasons is Ayrton Senna *(below)* whose tenure was brief in 1994 before a fatal accident at Imola. Williams have won seven drivers' titles and more than 110 races and continue to play a leading role in F1 today.

Keke Rosberg

David Coulthard

The Williams of Carlos Reutemann
chases the Brabham of Nelson
Piquet during the 1980 Dutch
Grand Prix.

Damon Hill

Juan Pablo Montoya

■ MERCEDES

The reigning World Champions have a racing heritage stretching back not only to the 1950s but, before the start of the World Championship in 1950, to the 1930s. Having been absent since the end of the Second World War, Mercedes returned halfway through the 1954 season and wiped the floor with his opponents, using streamlined cars that were peerless during the French Grand Prix on the fast straights of Reims *(this page)*. Following a tragedy in the 1955 Le Mans 24-Hours sports car race, Mercedes withdrew from motor racing, but not before Juan Manuel Fangio had dominated the championship. The German firm returned as an engine supplier in the 1990s, winning championships with McLaren before becoming a team in their own right once more in 2010. Fully prepared for a change in regulations at the start of 2014, Mercedes dominated F1 with Lewis Hamilton winning back-to-back titles and Nico Rosberg taking a third in 2016.

Nico Rosberg *(above, top right, bottom left)* **won Monaco three years in succession for Mercedes and took the Championship in 2016.**

Lewis Hamilton *(top left, centre, left and right)* **won successive world championships with Mercedes in 2014 and 2015.**

Michael Schumacher racing in Malaysia in 2012 *(bottom right)***. He spearheaded the return of Mercedes as a team in 2010.**

■ BENETTON

Having sponsored Tyrrell and Alfa Romeo, the Italian fashion family bought into F1 in a major way in 1985 by purchasing Toleman and transforming the small British team. Benetton, powered by BMW engines, scored their first win in Mexico in 1986, a one-off result largely through being on superior tyres on the day. Nelson Piquet *(right)* brought limited success, but it was not until a restructured team and the arrival of Michael Schumacher *(above right)* in late 1991 that Benetton began to enjoy consistent success. The German driver won the first of two back-to-back titles in 1994, the team boosted by a pair of wins for Johnny Herbert *(above left)* in 1994 and 1995. After accounting for nineteen of Benetton's twenty-seven victories, Schumacher's departure to Ferrari for 1996 marked the beginning of a decline in fortune for Benetton, the family selling out to Renault at the end of 2001.

THE CIRCUITS
TRIUMPH AND TRAGEDY ON F1'S COURSES

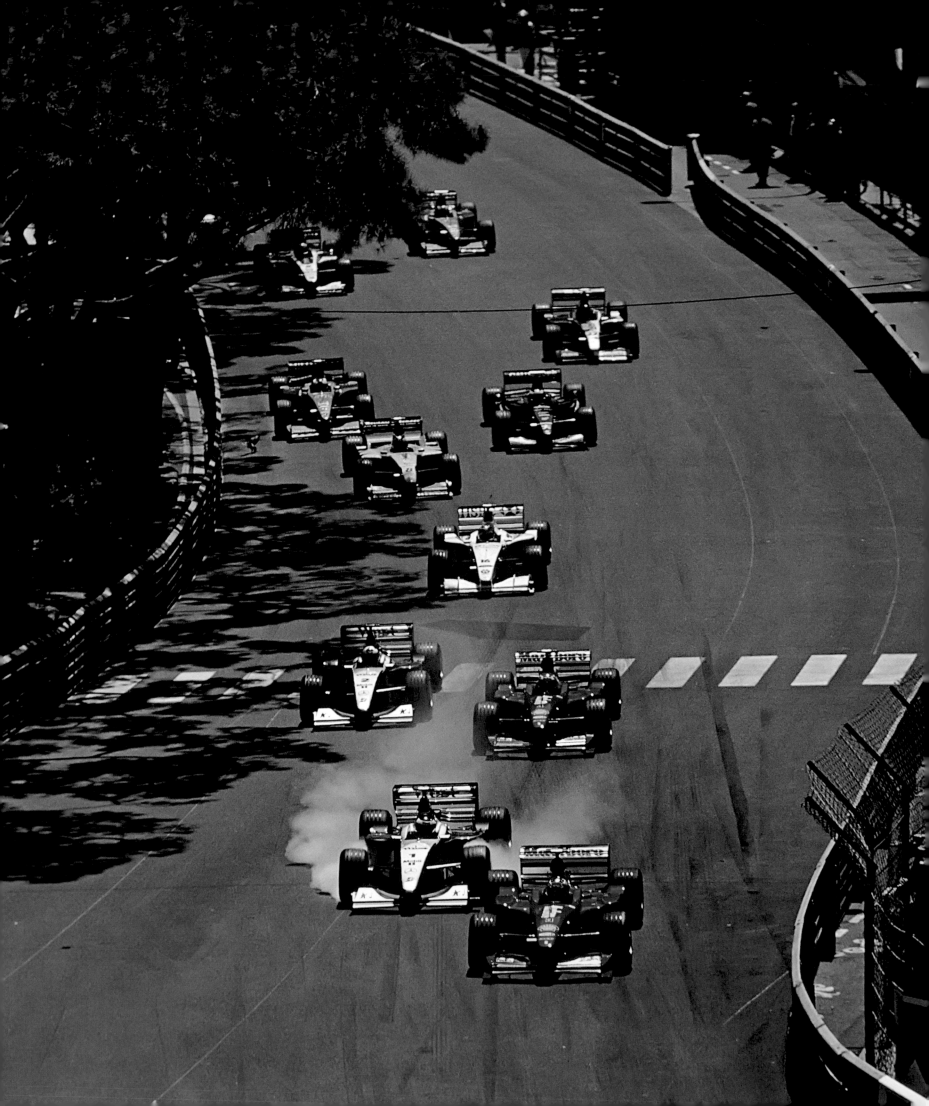

Previous pages
Best of both worlds for Ferrari at Suzuka in 2003 after Rubens Barrichello (with crash helmet) has won the Japanese Grand Prix and Michael Schumacher has become World Champion.

Left
Monaco: the most famous of them all. Mika Hakkinen locks his brakes behind Michael Schumacher as the Ferrari and McLaren-Mercedes lead the pack into the first corner at the start of the 1999 Monaco Grand Prix.

Overleaf
Top left **The starting grid at Monaco (shown in 1957) used to be on the straight that is now the pit lane run in the reverse direction.**

Top right **Heading off to the seaside: the first lap of the 1960 Dutch Grand Prix at Zandvoort.**

Bottom left **Riverside in California was used just once to stage the United States Grand Prix. The race gets under way in 1960.**

Bottom right **Spa-Francorchamps in Belgium is notorious for fickle weather. Jim Clark heads for victory with his Lotus-Climax in 1963.**

There have been more than seventy different race tracks used to stage Grands Prix since the start of the World Championship in 1950. Some have been used just once. Others, such as Monaco and Monza, have provided a perpetual showcase just as intoxicating and passionate as the sport itself.

The striking difference between these two traditional venues sums up the variety that makes F1 what it is. And the fact that both Monza and Monaco have been responsible for the writing of racing drivers' obituaries also underscores the tragedy that occasionally stalks the sport and tarnishes its best intentions, no matter where or what form the track may take.

Monza is a purpose-built high-speed circuit, established in 1922 in the Royal Park within a suburb of Milan. Monaco is the slowest on the F1 calendar thanks to the racing being constricted by narrow streets that make up arguably the best-known Grand Prix track in the world. The contrast may be stark and the challenge diverse but the end game is the same as it has always been; to finish first and score maximum championship points. Then move on to the next race track. And the one after that.

Variety has always been an essential part of F1's fabric. The first motoring competitions were staged more than 100 years ago with races from city to city. The inherent danger to spectators brought an awareness of the need for more control in the shape of a circuit that could be more easily managed and provide some form of crowd constraint. That said, public highways and byways continued to provide the easiest, if not the most socially convenient, form of race track, but permanent venues soon became popular and offered more potential for profit.

Nonetheless, when the World Championship was introduced, the seven-race calendar in 1950 was dominated, not by permanent fixtures, but by road and street tracks such as Spa-Francorchamps, Reims, Berne and, of course, Monaco. The diversity presented by these four ensured their presence: Spa utilising nine undulating miles of roads sweeping through the Belgian Ardennes; Reims being a flat and very fast triangle of straight roads amid corn fields to the west of the French city; Berne, a scary and relentless sequence of curves and high-speed corners through woods on the northern outskirts of the Swiss capital; and Monaco has been described above.

By their very nature, all four were bound to cause casualties. But, even allowing for a more relaxed approach to safety in the decade following the Second World War,

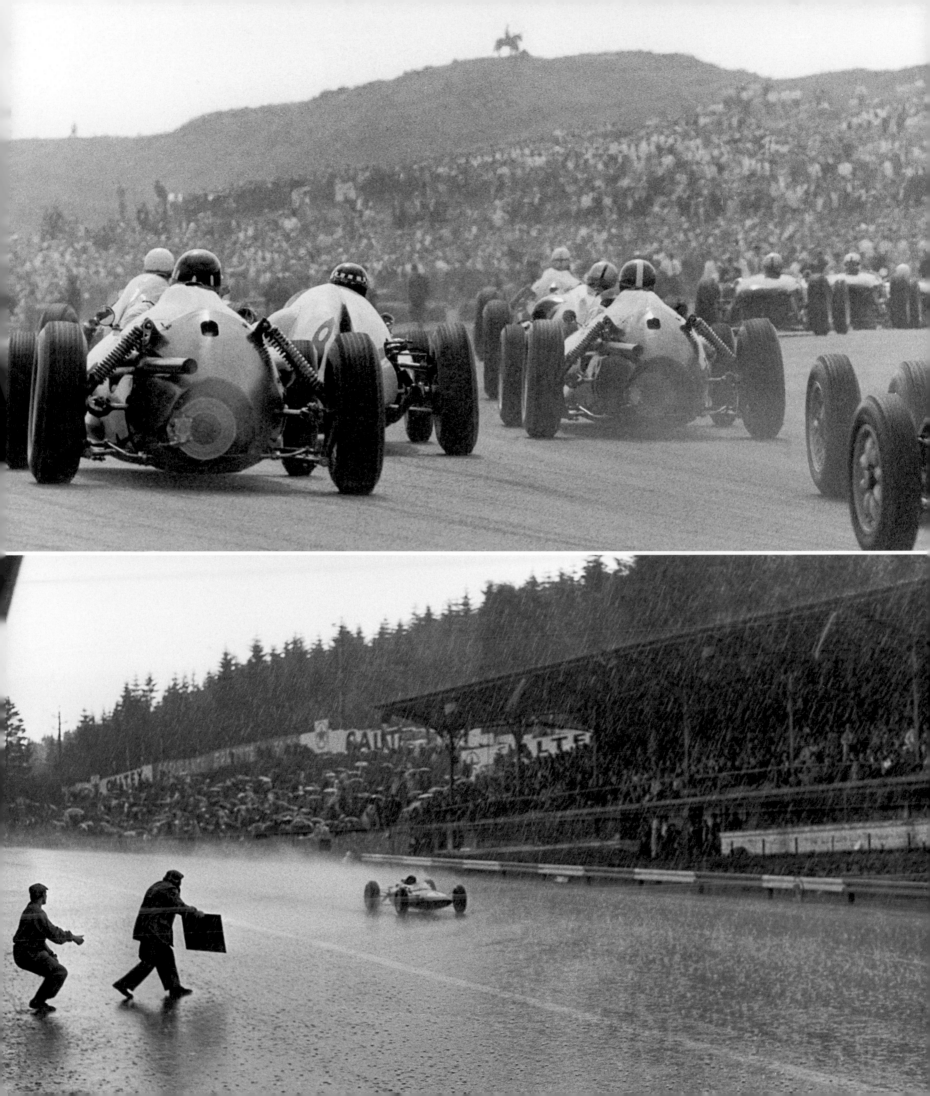

Berne in particular was considered excessively dangerous. The end of Grand Prix racing in Berne in 1955, however, was not due to the inherent risks but because motor racing was banned in Switzerland following the death of more than eighty spectators that year in the Le Mans 24-Hour sports car race.

Danger was not confined to circuits on public highways passing between trees. The Nürburgring, thought to be one of the greatest race tracks ever built when opened in 1926, was also one of the most hazardous. It could hardly be otherwise given that this leviathan snaked its way through the Eifel mountains for fourteen tortuous miles, with no two of more than 170 corners being the same. Not a year would pass without casualties, the situation made worse by the impossible task of marshalling this giant of a race track.

The same applied, albeit to a lesser degree, through the fast curves of Spa, and yet each track survived through the 1960s, despite a litany of sorrow. This in itself summed up the conflict of emotion that attended such majestic tracks. Paradoxically, the knowledge that an error could be severely punished brought a frisson of excitement as a driver measured up to the challenge of getting through these corners faster than anyone else. They were racing against the track just as much as their competitors.

Under different circumstances because of lower speeds, the same test of daring nevertheless applied to Monaco, where a wheel a fraction out of line would bring instant retirement against a wall or kerb. The wide grassy expanse of Silverstone – a former airfield – this most certainly was not.

It was an immediate means of measuring a driver's skill and precision – with the added ingredient of maintaining concentration throughout a race lasting, in the 1950s and 1960s, at least, for more than two hours, often in searing heat. The price of the smallest misjudgement could be horrific.

At Monaco in 1967, Lorenzo Bandini was carrying the hopes of Ferrari – and by association, the whole of Italy – as he chased the leader with 19 of the 100 laps remaining. A tiny miscalculation had massive consequences as he clipped the high-speed chicane leading to the harbour front. Thrown from its course, the Ferrari hit straw bales lining the outside of the corner, overturned and caught fire. Even with marshals in close proximity, Bandini could not be extricated and died in hospital days later. There have been no fatalities at Monaco since.

In fact, the sport's terrible record improved massively as F1 came to terms with the fact that race tracks needed to offer the best possible protection and medical support should a driver crash – not necessarily through any fault of his own. From having close to one fatality every month during the 1968 season, Grands Prix ran for twelve years without tragedy until the 1994 San Marino Grand Prix when two drivers were killed. The fact that one of them was Ayrton Senna, a three-time World Champion and six-time winner at Monaco, brought home the fact that circuits could never be completely safe.

But that has not stopped the search for perfection. If anything, it has accelerated it. The sport's governing body, the FIA, examines every detail of every accident, fatal or not. Circuits and facilities are improved continuously.

Spa-Francorchamps remains proof that this can be done without compromising the very reason a driver snuggles into the cockpit, has his seat harness pulled painfully tight, closes his visor, grips the wheel and prepares to take on the race track. Spa was heavily revised in 1983 and yet retains much of its original character. It is a place where a hint of sweat on a driver's brow and a wide-eyed expression says everything about man and machine versus race track. It's about flirting with danger and embracing triumph. Just as it always was.

Above
Nigel Mansell sweeps through the exit of Paddock Hill Bend on his way to victory with the Williams-Honda at Brands Hatch in 1985.

Opposite
Ayrton Senna's Lotus-Renault charges down the hill at Spa-Francorchamps in 1985 and prepares to tackle Eau Rouge, one of the classic corners in F1.

■ FRANCE

There have been more Grand Prix tracks in France than in any other European country. Reims *(left and p.194 bottom)* was an obvious choice when the championship was instigated in 1950, the flat triangle of public roads having been used for racing since 1932. Jim Clark and Lotus won in 1963 *(p.195, bottom and top right)*, three years before Reims was deemed unsafe because of the extremely high speeds. Rouen, a fast but very different type of road circuit, was first used in 1952 *(Ascari's winning Ferrari pictured p.194, top right)*, the cobbled hairpin being a feature of this picturesque but dangerous track *(Fangio's Maserati negotiates the hairpin p.194, top left, on his way to victory in 1957)*. When introduced to the F1 calendar in 1965, stunning roads around an extinct volcano above Clermont-Ferrand were popular among drivers, if not the mechanics, forced to use a rudimentary paddock. Here you see the March and BRM teams cheek by jowl *(p.196)* in 1970, two years before the final Grand Prix was dominated by Chris Amon's Matra *(p.197)* until the luckless New Zealander suffered a puncture. A purpose-built circuit at Paul Ricard may have been considered safer when first used in 1971 but the track, high above the Mediterranean coast, produced a spectacular incident in 1989 *(p.198)* when Mauricio Gugelmin misjudged his braking at the first corner and became airborne, the turquoise March wiping off the rear wing from Nigel Mansell's Ferrari as Thierry Boutsen's Williams-Renault (number 5) locked a front brake in avoidance. No one was hurt.

Far left
The March and BRM teams cheek by jowl at Clermont-Ferrand in 1970 *(top)*. The Ferraris of Didier Pironi and Patrick Tambay at the start of the 1982 French Grand Prix at Paul Ricard *(middle)*. Chris Amon's Matra powers through one of the many bends at Clermont-Ferrand in 1972 *(bottom)*.

Left
Paul Ricard is scheduled to return to the F1 calendar in 2018 *(top)*. Patriotic colours at Magny-Cours.

The alarmingly-forward driving position in 1982 demonstrated by Jacques Laffite's Ligier-Matra at Paul Ricard *(above)*. In an early battle for fourth place at Paul Ricard in 1978, Patrick Tambay's McLaren leads Ronnie Peterson's Lotus, the McLaren of James Hunt, Alan Jones in a Williams and the Wolf of Jody Scheckter *(right)*.

Overleaf
The purpose-built track at Paul Ricard produced a spectacular crash on the first lap in 1989 – fortunately, no one was hurt.

■ MONACO

This is the most famous race track in the world, if only because 70 per cent of what you see today was used for the first Grand Prix in 1929. The setting could not be more glamorous, from the steep climb towards the Hotel de Paris and the Casino, to the tunnel and the dash along the waterfront, the entire glittering scene overlooked by the Royal Palace.

The Mercedes of Stirling Moss (6) and Juan Manuel Fangio lead the pack through Gasworks Hairpin, the first corner in 1955.

Graham Hill tweaks his famous moustache with the bearded Jo Bonnier and Raymond Mays, the boss of BRM, in the background.

Moss looks on as Mike Hawthorn receives a light.

Surtees, Hill and Bandini in 1965.

Jackie Stewart congratulates his BRM team-mate Hill after winning in 1965.

The Maserati (28) of eventual winner Stirling Moss fights with the Ferrari (22) of Eugenio Castellotti from the start in 1956 *(above)*.

The backdrop may have changed, but the hairpin remains exactly as it was; the Ferraris of Lorenzo Bandini and John Surtees negotiate the tightest corner in F1 in 1965 *(top left)* and Chris Amon's March leads the Brabham of Jack Brabham, Jacky Ickx's Ferrari and the Matra of Jean-Pierre Beltoise away from the hairpin in 1970 *(top right)*.

Hill's winning Lotus is parked by the kerb in what was the pit lane in 1968 *(right)*. The original track was shorter than today, the start and finish area being where the pit lane is presently located. The addition around the swimming pool in 1973 began just after Tabac *(middle left, being negotiated by Luigi Musso's Ferrari in 1958)* and allowed the pits to be removed to safety from the side of the main start and finish straight.

Ayrton Senna's McLaren-Ford
climbs the hill in 1993 on his
way to the last of a record six
wins at Monaco.

David Coulthard won twice in
the Principality.

Nico Rosberg points his Mercedes
up the hill towards Casino.

The Williams of Valtteri Bottas
kicks up sparks.

Kimi Räikkönen's Ferrari tackles
Tabac in 2015.

■ ITALY

The Italian Grand Prix is all about the madness of Monza, captured perfectly in 1970 as Clay Regazzoni's winning Ferrari was engulfed as an enthusiastic mob invaded the track *(below)*, the huge numbers indicating many had actually climbed the fence before the race had finished. This shot also catches the historic sense of the famous autodrome, opened in 1922 with the banking, no longer used, arcing across the background. The flat-out nature of the long straights has produced epic battles with Italian red cars usually in the midst of them.

Juan Manuel Fangio's Maserati leads the Ferraris of Alberto Ascari and Giuseppe Farina in 1953.

A happy Jim Clark, victor at Monza in 1963.

Fangio drifts his Maserati 250F while chasing the Vanwall of Tony Brooks in 1957, the same pair poised on the grid before the start.

Overleaf
A study in concentration as Stirling Moss prepares to start the same race in his Vanwall.

Sebastian Vettel prepares for
the start at Monza in 2015.
The emergence of Imola as an
alternative saw the Italian Grand
Prix shift to the picturesque track
in the province of Bologna in
1980 before assuming the title
San Marino Grand Prix in 1981.

The atmosphere was no less passionate despite Ferrari not being part of a battle between the McLaren-Hondas of Ayrton Senna and Alain Prost in 1988.

Ferrari adulation at the exit of Imola's Tosa corner.

Overleaf
There was little in motorsport to match the pulsating atmosphere on the hillside at Imola.

Jenson Button produced stirring performances in the BAR-Honda at Imola.

Sadly, Imola will also be remembered for the death of Senna. Memorabilia in tribute adorns the fence at Tamburello, the corner where the Brazilian's Williams-Renault crashed on 1 May 1994.

Michael Schumacher brought joy to the home crowd with no fewer than six wins for Ferrari.

■ HOLLAND

The seaside track at Zandvoort was hugely popular from the moment it hosted the first Dutch Grand Prix in 1952, the sand dunes forming excellent viewing points. Located a train ride from Amsterdam, the race became a regular feature of the F1 calendar and attracted spectators from France, Belgium and Germany, as well as from across the English Channel. British fans were thrilled to witness James Hunt score his first Grand Prix win after his Hesketh-Ford held off Niki Lauda's Ferrari in 1975. The long main straight, illustrated in the start shot from 1965 *(top left)*, contributed to close racing as cars braked heavily for the first corner. In 1966 Jack Brabham led Jim Clark away from that corner *(top, middle)*. Twelve years later, Mario Andretti and Lotus team-mate Ronnie Peterson dominated the race, 1985 providing a livelier Grand Prix as Alain Prost *(middle)* battled with his McLaren team-mate Niki Lauda. René Arnoux's Renault led the field at the start in 1980 *(bottom, right)*.

■ PORTUGAL

Jim Clark's set expression *(right)* summed up a rare driving error as the Scotsman walked away from his damaged Lotus in Porto in 1960. Attempting to take the first corner flat out during practice while avoiding the tramlines that were part of the street circuit, Clark clipped a kerb and spun into the straw bales. The car was patched up and Clark went on to score his first podium finish the next day. The street circuit, with its mixed surfaces and cobblestones, was only used twice, one more time than a road circuit at Monsanto near Lisbon where Dan Gurney is pictured *(above)* in his Ferrari on his way to third place in 1959. Portugal would be without a Grand Prix until the upgrading of Estoril in 1984. This permanent track would stage thirteen Grands Prix and prove popular for testing.

Niki Lauda raises an arm in triumph at Estoril in 1984, second place being good enough to give the McLaren driver the championship by half a point.

The Benettons of Alessandro Nannini and Thierry Boutsen are prepared in the cramped garages in 1988.

Gerhard Berger's Ferrari raises sparks on the narrow and bumpy main straight in 1989.

■ HUNGARY

F1's first venture into an Eastern bloc country in 1986 saw the introduction of the Hungarian Grand Prix at the Hungaroring. The purpose-built track was tight and twisting, the only overtaking place of note being into the first corner, where the Ferraris of Rubens Barrichello and Michael Schumacher led the Williams-BMW of Ralf Schumacher in 2002 *(right)*. Although the races tend to be processional, the Hungaroring has set statistical landmarks by settling the championship twice (Nigel Mansell in 1992 and Michael Schumacher 2001) as well as listing several first-time winners (Damon Hill in 1993, Fernando Alonso in 2003, Jenson Button in 2006 and Heikki Kovalainen in 2008).

■ GERMANY

The German Grand Prix has been staged on four different circuits, none more infamous than the Nürburgring Nordschleife, twisting and turning for fourteen miles through the Eifel mountains. Opened in 1926, the circuit joined the World Championship trail in 1951 and remained on it until deemed too dangerous following Niki Lauda's near-fatal crash in 1976. In 1957 the race produced one of the most mesmeric performances of all when Juan Manuel Fangio *(below)* chased, caught and overtook the Ferraris of Peter Collins and Mike Hawthorn after making a pit stop. Fangio posed in his Maserati (number 1) alongside Hawthorn's Ferrari *(left)* before the start. The field gets away in 1956 *(far left)* and John Surtees takes his first Grand Prix victory for Ferrari in 1963 *(below, left)*.

Jim Clark (1) leads Graham Hill's
BRM into the first corner of the
1965 Grand Prix *(above)*, Clark
going on to win, his Lotus-Climax
casting a shadow in 1964 as the
circuit weaves its way through
the forest *(right)*.

Overleaf
When the Nordschleife fell from
favour, and before a new track
was built alongside, the Grand
Prix moved to Hockenheim,
where Rubens Barrichello scored
an emotional maiden victory in
his Ferrari in 2000.

■ SPAIN

Spain has been part of F1's fabric since the early days with no fewer than six different tracks staging the Grand Prix. Jarama, used nine times between 1968 and 1981 *(top row: left, centre left and centre right)*, was arguably the least popular, the 1970 race being marred by a fire when two cars collided, leaving victory to the blue March of Jackie Stewart. Gilles Villeneuve scored a spectacular and unexpected win in 1981 when he managed to withstand huge pressure and hold everyone back with the cumbersome Ferrari (number 27). Jerez *(top row, right; bottom row, left)* was used seven times between 1986 and 1997 before the Spanish race found a more permanent home outside Barcelona at Circuit de Catalunya. The Williams-Renault of Nigel Mansell and Ayrton Senna's McLaren-Honda engaged in an epic wheel-to-wheel contest at the first race in 1991 *(above)*. McLaren's Lewis Hamilton

and Fernando Alonso *(bottom row, centre right)* sprayed the
champagne after finishing second and third in 2007, with happier
times for the home hero as Alonso greeted his fans after winning
for Ferrari in 2013 *(bottom row, right)*.

■ BELGIUM

Despite ten visits to Zolder, Spa-Francorchamps is considered to be the spiritual home of the Belgian Grand Prix. The awesome circuit in the Ardennes was first used for a Grand Prix in 1925, its nine-mile length causing havoc in 1966 when the race started in the dry and competitors ran into a rainstorm a quarter of the way round the first lap. It was wet for the start in 1965 *(opposite bottom left)* as the field left the downhill grid and headed into Eau Rouge before the steep, curving climb through the trees towards Les Combes. The Ferraris of Phil Hill and Ricardo Rodriguez fight it out in 1962 *(opposite top, left)*. The Cooper-Maserati of Jo Siffert crests the rise at Eau Rouge in 1967 *(opposite top, right)*. Spa had

become the fastest road circuit in use by 1960 when two British drivers were killed in separate accidents. Growing concern over safety brought a halt to Spa's inclusion on the calendar after the 1970 Grand Prix, but a first-rate piece of modernisation saw the race return in 1983. The circuit had virtually been cut in half but the atmosphere and challenge remained, particularly the swoop through Eau Rouge. The climb to Les Combes *(above)* had been straightened to allow speeds approaching 200 mph, contributing to Spa's continuing reputation as a fast and demanding track. Nigel Mansell *(top, right)*, heads back to the pits after retiring in 1991.

■ JAPAN

Japan has used three circuits: Suzuka, Mount Fuji and Aida. Suzuka stands head and shoulders above not only the other two Japanese venues but just about every other race track on the F1 calendar. It is unique in being the only figure-of-eight layout in Grand Prix racing thanks to a design generated in the early 1960s, one that made Suzuka a fascinating and difficult proposition for the drivers when the Grand Prix arrived in 1987. By comparison, Fuji is relatively simple and was used in 1976 and 1977, the first visit being famous for settling a season-long championship battle between James Hunt and Niki Lauda during a race run in atrocious conditions. There was heavy rain when the Grand Prix returned in 2007 *(opposite, top)*, the following year being the final visit to Fuji before it reverted to Suzuka. Being at or near the end of the season, Suzuka has seen the crowning of several champions, often under controversial circumstances, none more so than in 1990 when Alain Prost and Ayrton Senna collided at the first corner *(top, right)*. Nigel Mansell and Williams team-mate Riccardo Patrese (6) run neck-and-neck into the first corner in 1992 *(bottom, right)*, Mansell having gone off at the same corner in 1991 *(bottom, left)*. Mansell's Williams chases the Ferrari of Jean Alesi in 1994 *(opposite, left)*. Mika Hakkinen wins the championship for McLaren in 1998 *(opposite, right)*.

■ CANADA

Canada has hosted a round of the championship since 1967, starting with Mosport Park and moving to Saint-Jovite the following year, where it ran twice. The race stayed at Mosport until 1977, by which time a new venue on a man-made island in the Saint Lawrence River was ready to become the permanent home for the Canadian Grand Prix. Despite a flat and straightforward profile, the Circuit Gilles Villeneuve (named after Canada's favourite motor racing son) is a tough proposition, mistakes being punished by the close proximity of concrete walls. It is a popular venue thanks to its location close by the city of Montreal and a knowledgeable and enthusiastic crowd. Originally placed at the end of the season, Montreal settled the championship in favour of Alan Jones in 1980, but a move to the summer months was favoured because of better weather conditions.

The Benetton of Michael
Schumacher *(right)* leads Damon
Hill's Williams *(left)* into the first
corner during their championship
battle in 1995.

Montreal was the scene of Lewis
Hamilton's first Grand Prix win
in 2007, and another victory in
2012. In 2005, Kimi Räikkönen
took his only victory in Canada,
the McLaren driver finishing
ahead of Ferrari's Michael
Schumacher *(right)*.

■ AUSTRIA

A simple but fiercely bumpy airfield track at Zeltweg provided a spartan venue for Austria's first championship Grand Prix in 1964. The circuit was never used again and when a brand new track was built in the foothills overlooking the airfield, the comparison could not have been more dramatic. Ready for a Grand Prix in 1970, the Österreichring was a magnificent collection of fast, sweeping curves making full use of the natural majesty of its surroundings in Styria. Thousands of spectators from across the Italian border enjoyed a dream result when Jacky Ickx and Clay Regazzoni finished first and second for Ferrari. Eighteen Grands Prix were staged here until the track was considered too remote a location

and out of step with the changing commercial requirements of F1. The average speed had risen to more than 150 mph and concern had grown over the lack of run-off at quick corners such as the Bosch Kurve *(left)*. A ten-car pile up on the narrow pit straight at the start of the race in 1987 added to the pressure to have the race removed from the calendar. The Grand Prix returned ten years later to a shortened track known as the A1-Ring, where the race was staged until 2003 and included two wins for Michael Schumacher *(right)*. After much debate over future plans, the site was bought by Red Bull and upgraded in readiness for a round of the championship in 2014.

■ MEXICO

A passion for motorsport in Mexico was answered in 1961 by the building of an impressive track within Magdalena Mixhuca, a municipal park in the suburbs of Mexico City. Granted a round of the World Championship in 1963, the race soon established itself as a welcome part of the calendar *(above: Jo Siffert takes his Lotus-BRM to ninth place in 1963)*. The Mexican Grand Prix settled the championship in favour of John Surtees in 1964 and Graham Hill in 1968. Hill led Chris Amon's Ferrari on the first lap in 1967, but victory would go to Hill's Lotus team-mate, Jim Clark, lying third behind Amon *(right, above)*. The previous year's race was won by the Cooper-Maserati of Surtees, seen leading Jack Brabham's crossed-up Brabham-Repco at the hairpin *(right, below)*. The Mexican race would not be without its controversy, particularly in 1970 when the overenthusiastic crowd encroached onto the edge of the track and a large dog was fatally hit by Jackie Stewart's Tyrrell. Removed from the calendar, the race was revived on a shorter version of the track between 1986 and 1992, returning once more with further revisions in 2015.

■ BRAZIL

The emergence of Emerson Fittipaldi as Brazil's first World
Champion in 1972 accelerated the desire to stage a Grand Prix in
his home country. The obvious choice was Interlagos, a permanent
track opened in 1940 and twisting and turning within itself on
land on the edge of São Paulo's sprawling southwest suburbs
(above, Jean-Pierre Jarier's Shadow-Ford in 1975). Appropriately,
Fittipaldi's Lotus-Ford won the first championship Grand Prix in
1973, Interlagos staging the race until 1980, by which time it was
deemed to be too bumpy and dangerous. Jacarepaguá *(p.250,
top row, left)*, a new track near Rio de Janeiro, was favoured from
1981 until the rise of Ayrton Senna from São Paulo prompted
a major facelift at Interlagos in readiness for a return in 1990.
The circuit length had been reduced by almost half but the huge
enthusiasm of the Brazilian fans remained and often needed
cooling down in the torpid heat of race day *(left)*. Passion would
run even higher if a Brazilian driver was in the reckoning, as was
the case when Felipe Massa *(p.250, bottom right, and p.251)*
fought with Lewis Hamilton for the title in 2008, only to lose on
the final lap.

Nigel Mansell heads for a
surprise victory for Ferrari at
Rio de Janeiro in 1989.

Michael Schumacher blasts his
Ferrari away from the pit box
at Interlagos in 1999.

The Williams of Damon Hill
(left) sits it out with Rubens
Barrichello's Jordan into the first
corner of the 1996 Brazilian
Grand Prix at Interlagos.

Felipe Massa savours the home
support after winning the 2006
Brazilian Grand Prix for Ferrari.

Kimi Raikkonen celebrates winning the world title at the final race of the 2007 season at Interlagos.

■ MALAYSIA

A desire to promote Malaysia as an international force led to the construction of a 3.4-mile track at Sepang, close by a new airport serving Kuala Lumpur. Costing 12 million US dollars, the venue was well received when the F1 teams arrived for the first Grand Prix in 1999. The track utilised the rolling landscape to include corners of every type and two wide straights with tight turns at the end of each to encourage overtaking. The first corner was unique in that it turned in on itself initially and offered drivers different lines to help promote close racing. Apart from the G-forces generated by several of the quick corners, drivers had to cope with high levels of humidity, making this one of the toughest races on the calendar.

Sebastian Vettel (below) **leads the Ferraris of Fernando Alonso and Felipe Massa at the start in 2013.**

■ SWITZERLAND

Switzerland's history of Grand Prix tracks is a slim volume thanks largely to motor racing being banned within the country's borders following the death of more than eighty spectators during the 1955 Le Mans 24-Hour race. The one track the country had used to stage five championship Grands Prix between 1950 and 1954 was also deemed too dangerous. The Bremgarten circuit was made up of roads running through a forest on the northern edge of Berne. With no straights worthy of the name, the 4.5-mile track formed a relentless series of curves and high-speed corners made even more difficult by constant changes of surface that would become treacherous in the wet. Add the close proximity of trees on both

sides of a track with an average speed of around 100 mph and it was no surprise to find fatalities were common. The final race in 1954 was won by the Mercedes of Juan Manuel Fangio (below), the rudimentary crowd safety arrangements clearly shown. The title 'Swiss Grand Prix' was given to a round of the World Championship at Dijon in France in 1982, the French Grand Prix having been run at Paul Ricard earlier that year.

■ UNITED KINGDOM

Chosen as the first-ever round of the World Championship in 1950, the British Grand Prix has been a kingpin in the series, never failing to host a round, with Silverstone being the constant throughout. Aintree was the first alternative, the roads around the famous Grand National horse race course being used five times between 1955 and 1962. Stirling Moss scored his first Grand Prix win driving for Mercedes in 1955 *(above)*, the sun shining that day, unlike the wet 1961 race *(far right)* as the field lined up in view of Aintree's imposing grandstands. Juan Manuel Fangio *(right)* won the British Grand Prix once and finished a close second to Moss in 1955. One of the greatest contests occurred at Silverstone in 1969 *(overleaf)* as the Lotus-Ford of Jochen Rindt and Jackie Stewart's Tyrrell-Ford (number 3) blasted off the line at the start of a wheel-to-wheel tussle that would last for over an hour, the pair lapping the field, including the McLaren-Ford of Denny Hulme (number 5).

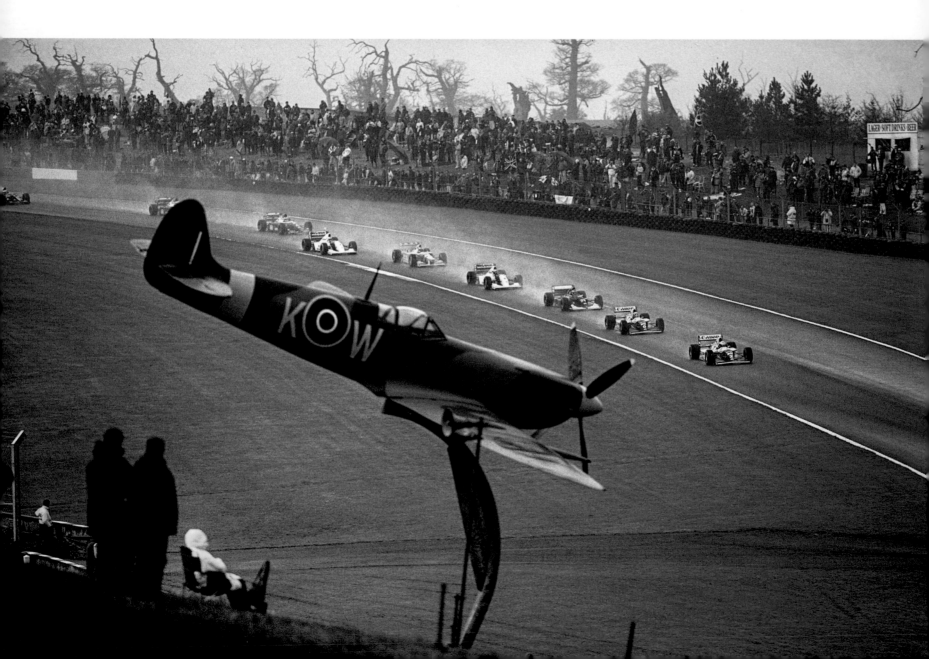

Brands Hatch hosted the race fourteen times, starting in 1964 and including 1986 *(below, Nelson Piquet's Williams-Honda leads the pack through Paddock Hill Bend)*. **Donington Park** *(below, left)* hosted a championship round just once, the 1993 European Grand Prix being memorable for a stunning drive by Ayrton Senna. The Brazilian's McLaren-Ford lay fourth behind the Williams-Renaults of Alain Prost and Damon Hill and Karl Wendlinger's Sauber not long after the start of the opening lap. Senna would be leading at the end of it. Jack Brabham *(above, left)* won the British Grand Prix for Cooper at Aintree on his way to the first World Championship for a rear-engine car in 1959.

■ UNITED STATES

With no fewer than ten different venues since 1959, the United States Grand Prix has tried everything from permanent tracks to street circuits and an adaption of the famous Indianapolis 500 oval. Following brief visits to Sebring in Florida and Riverside in California, Watkins Glen became the most successful, the purpose-built track in New York State being used twenty times before it was no longer considered suitable in 1981. In 1982, there were three Grands Prix in the USA: on the streets of Long Beach and in a converted car park in Las Vegas in the west, and in downtown Detroit *(above)*, a street circuit that went on to host the US Grand Prix East seven times. For various reasons – mainly finance and an inability to meet required standards – all three faded, to be replaced by unsuccessful attempts on the streets of Phoenix and Dallas. Indianapolis, never totally satisfactory, lasted for eight years until, finally, a brand new circuit near Austin in Texas appeared to answer all the questions when introduced in 2012, the race being won by the McLaren-Mercedes of Lewis Hamilton *(right)*.

The Ferrari crew rush to celebrate
the first of five victories
for Michael Schumacher at
Indianapolis.

Sebastian Vettel's Red Bull started
from pole at Austin in 2012.

The McLarens of Ayrton Senna
(right) and Alain Prost lead off in
1989 at the first of three Grands
Prix at Phoenix.

The distinctive Detroit skyline as
Ayrton Senna and Lotus prepare
for victory in 1986.

Austin's Circuit of the Americas
was a welcome addition in 2012.

■ AUSTRALIA

Grands Prix in Australia may have been limited to just two
venues across more than thirty years but each has been
considered an outstanding success. Adelaide set new standards
for a temporary track when introduced to the calendar in 1985,
the South Australian venue settling the championship in a
spectacular manner for Benetton's Michael Schumacher in 1994. A
heavyweight political battle saw the state of Victoria wrench the
country's Grand Prix away from Adelaide to Melbourne in 1996,
switching from the end to the beginning of the year in the process.
Jacques Villeneuve *(left)* caused a sensation on his F1 debut by
taking pole position in his Williams-Renault in 1996, while Michael
Schumacher *(above, in 1999)* won four times for Ferrari.

■ SINGAPORE

Singapore delivered high standards when it arrived on the F1 scene in 2008 and not only established a challenging track on the streets of the business district alongside Marina Bay but also chose to become the first Grand Prix to be run at night. Powerful overhead lights successfully replicated daylight conditions for the drivers while producing a spectacular sight as the three-mile combination of boulevards and highways passed iconic landmarks such as the City Hall and the cricket ground, as well as crossing the ancient Anderson Bridge. A bumpy surface, angular corners and sapping humidity made this a tough test for the drivers in a race lasting an hour and three-quarters. A contract extended until 2017 was proof of the popularity and success of such a unique addition to the calendar.

INDEX

ACKNOWLEDGEMENTS

I would first like to thank my father, Bernard Cahier. This book is the result of a father and son collaboration, and even though my father is sadly no longer with us, he was by my side every day when working on this beautiful book. Searching through the negatives of the incredible, glorious days of Grand Prix Racing, I could feel his strong presence imbedded in the gelatine of the black and white films which I was scanning. He was behind the camera, and inside the film.

I would also like to thank Lucy Warburton from Aurum Press, my Editor, who was curious enough to search and discover the unique photographs from the Cahier Archive, and brave enough to push and make this book happen. What a great idea that was!

Finally, a big thank you to Sir Jackie Stewart for writing his heartfelt foreword to *Formula One: The Pursuit of Speed*. As it happened, I took my first photos of Formula 1 racing in Monza 1965, when I was a twelve-year-old boy and he won his first ever Grand Prix. Ever since those days, the Stewart and the Cahier families have remained friends, and nobody was in a better position to write the foreword than Jackie.

Brimming with creative inspiration, how-to projects and useful information to enrich your everyday life, Quarto Knows is a favourite destination for those pursuing their interests and passions. Visit our site and dig deeper with our books into your area of interest: Quarto Creates, Quarto Cooks, Quarto Homes, Quarto Lives, Quarto Drives, Quarto Explores, Quarto Gifts, or Quarto Kids.

First published in Great Britain
2017 by Aurum Press an imprint of The Quarto Group
The Old Brewery
6 Blundell Street
London N7 9BH

Original edition first published by Aurum Press in 2016
This updated edition published by Aurum Press in 2017

Photography copyright © The Cahier Archive 2016, 2017
Text copyright © Maurice Hamilton 2016, 2017
Foreword © Sir Jackie Stewart 2016

ISBN 978 1 78131 728 0

10 9 8 7 6 5 4 3 2 1
2021 2020 2019 2018 2017

Designed by Ashley Western
Printed in China